Making a Difference:

Cuff's Guide for
MUNICIPAL
LEADERS

A survival guide for elected officials

GEORGE B. CUFF

brought to you by the publishers of

THE MAGAZINE TRUSTED BY MUNICIPAL DECISION-MAKERS SINCE 1891

National Library of Canada Cataloguing in Publication

Cuff, George B.

Making a difference: Cuff's guide for municipal leaders: a survival guide for elected officials / George B. Cuff.

ISBN 0-919779-62-X

1. Municipal government – Canada. 2. Municipal officials and employees – Canada. I. Title. II. Title: Cuff's guide for municipal leaders. III. Title: Guide for municipal leaders.

JS1715.C83 2002   352.14'0971
C2002-904962-8

Published in Canada by
Municipal World Inc.
Box 399, Station Main
St. Thomas, Ontario N5P 3V3

(Union, Ontario N0L 2L0)

mwadmin@municipalworld.com
www.municipalworld.com

ITEM 0059

Municipal World — Reg. T.M. in Canada, Municipal World Inc.

CONTENTS

Preface

The completion of this text on local government has been both a significant task as well as the fulfillment of a personal goal of several years ago. After writing over 50 articles on matters of interest to municipalities over the past 25 years, I thought that it might be useful to put some of my observations into one source that could then be both used as well as updated by others involved in this fascinating field. As well, I found that some of my assignments required me to reiterate key background points on some of these matters in virtually every report. While this seemed necessary to set the stage for each report, it also became a difficult matter to make each one somewhat different than the other.

My observations are, in reality, a synopsis of what I have observed as a municipal department head (now years ago), an elected official for 12 years, and as a consultant – firstly with a provincial government for two years, and since as a management consultant for the past 24 years. These observations likely reflect the ideas of others with whom I have worked with over the years, articles that may have impacted my thinking, and comments made during the course of over 300 consulting engagements across Canada.

I am indebted to many people, and some quite specifically. My wife Arliss has both worked with me and supported me during my various endeavours. Our life together has had many twists and turns and yet has survived – due, in large measure, to her patience and forgiveness and to the grace of God. The input and assistance of two of my associates, Doug Plamping and Joel DeBlock, are much appreciated. The experience and wisdom of my consulting associates enable me to tackle a project of this magnitude. I am also very thankful to the editors of *Municipal World* for having been so helpful over the years in publishing my thoughts on matters germane to local government. In particular, I am appreciative to Susan Gardner and Mary Tully for their encouragement and advice relative to this text, which I am hopeful will be the first of a series on related matters. All observations and commentary are the responsibility of the author.

Chapter 1

INTRODUCTION

This text has been written for students and practitioners of local government, with those elected to office being the primary audience. This is not intended as a definitive text on the subject of being and staying elected. Rather, this guide offers some useful tips and principles with regard to the art of governance and to managing the relationship between governing bodies and their administrative managers.

Many of the problems that beset both elected and appointed officials are more the result of a lack of clarity regarding their respective roles than any other single factor. Thus, this represents an attempt to deal with these misconceptions – without, hopefully, creating more!

Be aware, though, that this is not a legal document. It is not legislation. It may not apply in specific circumstances in your jurisdiction. Although, where that may be so, attempt is made to keep the reader aware of that fact. Where there is any conflict between what I advise or comment on, and the legislation of your jurisdiction or the legal advice of your municipality's solicitor, I defer to those latter sources. In some instances (likely few), the legislation may have already changed (as much of it has recently, and continues to do so).

What Works

This book is based on what I believe works. It is drawn from the well of countless experiences, both personally and by others.

There are certain basic principles that I believe enable intelligent and appropriate decisions to be made. Thus, this book is not advocating simple solutions to each and every situation. Generally, such simple solutions simply do not work! In much of local government, as in life, if the decision-making process is properly thought through, the decision will generally be "right" or at least "appropriate" in that instance.

It is also not the intent of this book to bring into question each and every process currently utilized by your administration. In most instances, after having understood the background and culture of the organization, the way business is conducted in your community may very well be the most suitable. The determination of whether or not that is true is an assessment that must be made by you as an elected official and as an administrator. I would rather have the reader guided by an adage passed on to me by a mentor and friend, that the material herein is "something to be chewed, but not necessarily swallowed."

Chapter 2

SO, NOW YOU'VE BEEN ELECTED

Welcome to the very interesting, challenging and rewarding life of an elected official in local government. This experience will be unlike anything else in which you have been involved in terms of its variety, complexity and role change. There is little that can realistically prepare you for your new status as an elected official, although the experiences and surprises of life are as good a "school" as anything else one could do!

A Basic Problem

You are not expected to "manage" this "business." This has been the number one failure of elected officials across Canada. And, regardless of how often the same message is proclaimed at conferences and seminars, this will continue to be the case. Many people simply fail to learn by either their own experience or that of others. Being elected, in fact, requires the learning of a whole new way of seeing issues, and accepting a new role.

Regardless of how successful you have been in your own business or career, this experience offers few parallels. In many instances, you will be frustrated by the glacial speed of decision making, and wonder why everyone cannot move as quickly as you can – or perhaps thought you could. Perhaps you will argue that the municipality should be run as a business, only to recognize somewhat later that its basis as an institution representing the public requires that it approach decisions from a very different perspective.

Public Business

Public business must be done (and be seen to be done) publicly. While most candidates for municipal office are keen to support such a notion as they campaign, the tone often changes after the election. When, or if, the public's desire for information (or to be a party to the decision-making process) is vocalized and becomes insistent, then the public may be viewed by at least some members of council as a nuisance. Such an atti-

3

tude on behalf of a member of council (or council as a whole) generally signals an abbreviated tenure. This extremely important and sensitive matter is dealt with in more detail later in this book, particularly Chapter 7.

Becoming an elected official constitutes a new role. It will take some time to learn its intricacies. As a new member of council, you will be expected to "hit the ground running," but **not** as the expert on governance or on the administration of a municipality. To believe otherwise would reflect a lack of maturity and judgment. Most people have a genuine dislike for the "instant expert." There is nothing wrong with an admission of not being conversant with a particular topic or the arguments surrounding a contentious issue. The public is more likely to find such an admission refreshing.

Basic Principles of Elected Office

In order to be successful as an elected official, there are 15 basic principles that need to be understood:

1. The whole notion of elected office is based on two fundamental points: the rule of democratic representation, and the principle of accountability. The former speaks to the right of citizens to expect their elected members to reflect and represent their views on the issues; the latter speaks to the notion that those elected are accountable for their actions to those by whom they were elected.

2. The role of an elected official is unique. It is distinct and different from any other role. It needs to be learned and consciously applied if a council member is to be successful.

3. The public is, and always will be, the key to success. They alone determine the success and failure of political leaders.

4. Communicating out to the public is as important as receiving input from the public; both should to be valued.

5. Council is the servant of the public, and holds office at the pleasure of the public.

6. The will of the majority (as perceived by council) must be the most significant consideration in any decision making.

7. The opinions of the minority should be considered carefully before decisions are made.

8. Council and the administration should serve as a team, each with distinct roles, yet working together in the interests of the public.

9. Criticism of the administration, particularly on an individual basis, should never be tolerated by a council.

10. Council deals with the organization through one employee – the chief administrative officer (CAO). Any other course of action in attempting to guide the work of the administration should not be tolerated.

11. Council and its members cannot rest on their laurels. Each election campaign must be addressed as vigorously as the last campaign.

12. Each new council should determine its own priorities based on the input received during the campaign and subsequently (and supplemented by the advice of the administration), and should effectively communicate those priorities to the public.

13. Each council, regardless of the size of the community, needs to find ways of communicating its messages to the public, and should not rely exclusively on the media to perform that function.

14. Council members need to respect their colleagues on council as being the duly elected choices of the voters. While unanimous agreement need not be the case, respect for the opinions and votes of these colleagues is essential to the functioning of council.

15. Even leaders need a leader. All members of council are encouraged to uphold the office of head of council (or chief elected officer), even if they are in opposition to a particular statement or position taken by that official. Respect for each other is the hallmark of a mature council.

DISCUSSION GUIDE

1.   *What reasons prompted you to run for elected office at the municipal level?*

2.   *What have been your greatest surprises to date?*

3.   *Where do you turn to in attempting to find the answers to the problems facing your municipality?*

4.   *What has been your most difficult learning experience as a member of council?*

5.   *Which of the principles discussed in this Chapter do you consider to be most essential to the governance of your municipality and why?*

Chapter 3

THE NEED FOR ORIENTATION

Being elected is not just a new status – it represents the need for a whole new way of viewing issues and approaching decisions. It is both complex and simple: complex in the sense that the legislation and accompanying regulations are often quite difficult to digest without the benefit of some experience as a starting point; simple in that the decisions are generally those that can be viewed as common sense – which is generally not that common!

Prior to Election

The orientation process should begin before the election, not after the results are known. That is, each municipality should prepare basic candidate briefing material that sets out the roles of the head and members of council, and conveys the basic responsibilities of the municipality. Such preliminary briefing notes should also outline the basic elements of conflict of interest, so that "single issue" candidates, whose main concern with the current council may pertain to their own business, can determine if the pursuit of such an issue would place them in a conflict situation.

Critical Process

If each new council is to get off to a good start, it is essential that its administration prepare (although not necessarily conduct) an orientation process and materials. This should be guided by a policy of council that requires such a process and materials to be prepared in advance of an election. The role of facilitating this process with council may be contracted to an external party, at least insofar as guiding council in understanding its own roles is concerned.

The fact that such a council policy exists should ensure that an orientation process (and accompanying materials) are planned and prepared well in advance of an election. The actual orientation process should also be planned in advance (and all candidates for office notified), and should take place within two weeks of the election, or within one week of having been sworn into office. It is of little value if the orientation process is not held until some time after an election. By that time, council members will have already begun to develop their own way of doing things, and/or will have fallen into the same or similar patterns as their predecessors.

Each new council should be viewed as just that – new. That is, a new term of office has, by necessity, new members, even if those elected were on the previous council. While that will be difficult to understand or accept by some returning members, a council of seven with only one new member still has seven new relationships to form. This is the ideal time to begin anew.

Orientation Process

The orientation process for new members of a council should include a clear understanding of why it is being held, and what the intended results will be. Thus, those charged with planning such a session should:

1. Determine rationale/objectives for a council orientation.

2. Ensure that all members are aware of the planned orientation.

3. Try to get buy-in from participants beforehand.

4. Determine who is to attend and what roles they will play.

5. Recognize that new councils generally result in some degree of change.

6. Ensure that the focus is squarely on the roles of council. How will they govern? What were their issues during the campaign? What will be their priorities?

7. Determine who best to conduct the orientation sessions.

8. Refrain from making the session into "here's how we manage – isn't that exciting?"

9. Promote any necessary changes to the agenda, to council involvement with management, to the public profile of council, and to key council issues.

10. Focus on governance. What is it? Why is it important? How is it separate from the role of the CAO?

Orientation Session Agenda

The actual session should include:

1.0 Background Briefing

1.1 A welcome by the administration

1.2 Outline of key documents

1.3 Brief history of local government in the area

2.0 The Essence of Governance

2.1 Introduction to governance

2.2 Principles of governance

2.3 Review of basic roles and responsibilities of council and of its individual members (copy relevant sections of the Act and excerpts from other pertinent documents)

2.4 Review of the separate powers/duties of the mayor (copy relevant sections of the Act and excerpts from other pertinent documents)

3.0 Legal Briefing

3.1 Information provided by the municipality's solicitor or an external legal counsel on the key legal issues that may confront council, such as confidentiality, ethics, etc.

3.2 A legal description of roles and constraints on the exercise of individual powers

3.3 An updated status report on current outstanding legal issues

4.0 The "How To" of a Council Meeting

4.1 An outline of current style of council meetings

4.2 Choices available for change by this council

4.3 Role of a procedural bylaw

4.4 Timing of meetings

4.5 Protocol of meetings

4.6 The rudiments of presenting motions; seeking follow-up

4.7 Protocol regarding delegations; why it is important

4.8 Who attends meetings and why

4.9 The importance of preparation by council and CAO

4.10 Seating arrangements

4.11 Confidentiality; what it means; purpose of closed meetings

5.0 Role of the Administration

5.1 An assessment of the roles and powers of the CAO (copy relevant sections of the Act and excerpts from other pertinent documents)

5.2 Importance of role of the CAO

5.3 An overview of the roles of designated or statutory officers

5.4 An overview of the organizational structure

5.5 Brief introduction of department heads, including a summary of experience

5.6 Briefing on each department by department heads

5.7 Council's role in conducting performance appraisal of the CAO

5.8 Respond to questions

6.0 Overview of the Issues

6.1 Status report on the key issues

6.2 Policy issues of concern

6.3 Financial health of the municipality

6.4 Forecast of population/finances

6.5 Step-by-step presentation on the budget process

6.6 Role/importance/timing of the business plan

6.7 Relationship to neighbouring municipalities

6.8 Relationship to provincial government

6.9 Review of the roles and services of the relevant provincial and national associations

6.10 Tour of municipality (facilities; utilities; key roadways; key issues)

7.0 Close

7.1 An overview of the objectives and the intended results

7.2 An assessment by the participants

7.3 A discussion of future similar sessions

DISCUSSION GUIDE

1. *What process was followed by your municipality to ensure that you received a solid orientation to your new role?*

2. *What elements of your orientation did you consider to be the most useful to date?*

3. *What did you find out about governance that surprised you?*

4. *How will you and your colleagues on council set out your priorities for the municipality?*

Chapter 4

THE ART OF GOVERNANCE

Governance and management are uniquely different concepts, requiring the application of quite different skills. The former speaks more to understanding the will of the people and applying that to what needs to be done. The latter speaks to the application of sound administrative principles and practices in undertaking the action necessary to affect or implement the decisions of those governing.

Different Processes

While not totally exclusive from one another, the concepts of governance and management require mindsets that are quite distinct. The concept of management requires training in "how to undertake a certain act or set of actions." The concept of governance requires the vision to know "what is to be done." In all instances, governance must take precedence over management.

One of the principal components of an effective municipal organization is the awareness of the key roles and their impact on the system as a whole. Where such an understanding is lacking, the organization suffers. For example, in such an instance, council members may begin to act as though they have been hired to manage the system. Alternately, an administrator suffering from role confusion may presume that his or her length of experience, and presumably superior knowledge of municipal government entitles him or her to play the roles of both staff and council.

Defining Governance

Based on many years of counselling local government leaders across Canada, it is my firm belief that the concept of governance is not as clearly understood as it could be – neither by those governing nor by those administering the organization. This is evidenced by how little time is spent orienting council members to their elected responsibilities and, comparatively, how much more time is spent on showing council members what the administration is doing. It should not be surprising, then, if council members show far more aptitude for the roles of administration than governing, when so little time is accorded by those orchestrating orientation sessions to the actual art and significance of governing.

"Governance," in the context of local governments, could be defined as the process of exercising corporate leadership by the policy-making authority (i.e. council) on behalf of the public to the organization as a whole, in terms of its purpose, control and future and overseeing the organization to ensure that its mandate is achieved.

Applied Governance

One of the pressing (and generally unanswered) questions facing all elected and appointed leaders of organizations today is this: How can our leadership govern more effectively? This basic yet profound issue has confounded the leaders of our local and regional governments, and associated boards and agencies, as far back as I can recall, and remains the central question that inhibits (indeed plagues), such organizations.

Let us begin by examining the term "governance" to see what it really means, and how it can be applied to local government. The definition above begins by describing governance as a "process." That implies it requires ongoing attention, and is not a one-time project, wherein a manual of policies are adopted. It presumes that governance matters will regularly surface, and that the governing body is the only one to set the governance direction. Governing is an ongoing process that begins when a democratically-established body is brought into being, and when a group of people are elected (or appointed) to represent the views of those being served.

The definition also speaks of "leadership." While this word has many connotations, it generally denotes direction and authority. That is, someone must have the assigned authority to define where it is that the organization is going, and how it will proceed. In a local government, the role of leadership is deemed to fall to the mayor and council members in terms of the will of the people.

Further, the definition speaks of "policy making." Policy development is a process that, as described later, enables those in authority to guide the organization in accordance with their view of what is right in those circumstances. Policy development establishes the accepted norms of the organization, setting out what the leaders will do in a particular set of circumstances.

There is also an obligation on behalf of the governing authority to represent their constituents. In this instance, council is elected with the express purpose of representing the interests and rights of the public. This is a fundamental tenet of democratic governance. This requires that council become intimately aware of what the public interest may be defined to be in that community. This view by council may not always be understood or accepted by the administration, but it must be respected.

Finally, there is the matter of monitoring the organization's sustainability. The governing body must understand both *how* to monitor, and *what* to monitor. This is a critical aspect of governance, but one often overlooked until problems arise. Too often, monitoring or "oversight" is interpreted by elected officials as delving into the minutiae of the administration. This is inappropriate, as it blurs the lines of distinction between the two arms of the organization. The key for any elected body is to know what is to be monitored and how. That is, an elected body must understand what will directly impact the ongoing health of the organization, and what will contribute to the accomplishment of its goals. This is dealt with in Chapter 7.

Two key aspects of monitoring are important, and should be dealt with separately. These pertain to the obligation of a council to review and assess the performance of its chief administrative officer, as well as its own performance. There are techniques to fulfill both obligations, although these should be modified to fit local circumstances. Often, the process of council assessment is generally not well-known, largely ignored, or inadequate for the purpose intended. Such a process of self-examination needs to address the basic elements of council's own role and its annual objectives. A review such as this could serve as council's report card to the public, and a mechanism to seek public feedback. The diagram below shows the inter-relationship involved in this critical process of governance.

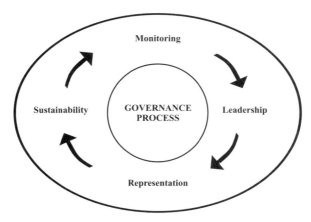

Monitoring

Sustainability   **GOVERNANCE PROCESS**   Leadership

Representation

Need for Effective Training

Provincial governments and municipal associations have been largely unsuccessful in identifying the role of the local governing body. In most instances, this has been due to an excessive concentration on the work of administrators. Provincial governments expend much of their energies in ensuring that local governments are being properly managed, while municipal associations focus on how best to lobby the government of the day for more money or improved (or less) legislation. Seldom is the spotlight placed squarely where it would do the most good, at least from a governance point of view.

Perhaps this shortcoming is due to the administrative background of those in leadership roles within the senior levels of the provincial bureaucracies. Perhaps we have collectively been lulled into unwittingly accepting the false premise that the governing body's involvement in "administrivia" is normal and, to a large extent, acceptable.

Frequently, the problem arises, or is at least compounded, by the absence of quality training of newly elected "governance" officials. Often, when training *is* provided, it is delivered by well-intentioned administrators or external advisors who convey, in serious tones, the importance of elected officials setting policy, and administrators carrying out that policy.

What Do We Do?

All of this is readily absorbed, but then begs a number of questions: "What do we, as elected people, actually do? What policies need to be set? Further, which ones do we already have? Are some required by legislation? Are we obligated to retain those policies that the prior council approved? Once we have considered the appropriate policies, what else can we do? When do we get into the interesting stuff? In other words, councillors may want to know when they get to delve into the work they have delegated to the administration. How this situation is handled at the outset will go a long way in determining the degree of success the administration will experience in keeping the two principal roles separate.

Value of Role Clarity

While municipalities face many governance issues, the seminal problem is one of role ambiguity. This can often lead to role conflict and/or role erosion, resulting in a weakening of authority. What do we mean by the term "governance?" How should a governing body govern? Which matters should be front and centre on any governance agenda?

Time spent discussing such questions at the outset of a governing body's term is worthwhile. Consider the time spent trying to pry such bodies away from roles that more logically (and often legally) reside in the administrative domain. Too often, the governing body is given a one hour to half day session on its roles – and, in many places, not even that. Then, it is introduced to how the administration "does the work" or the key issues of the day. The natural curiosity and often administrative or business backgrounds of those elected creates an inclination toward the "doing" functions, with little, if any, focus on governing. As a result, elected officials want to see how it all works – and except for the resistance of a very strong-willed administrator, that remains a focus for many of these individuals.

Governance Principles

In recent years, considerably more attention has been paid to this matter of governance. Perhaps this is due to problems that have beset many private sector corporations where boards of directors, when facing major financial disasters, are questioned as to what they knew and when they knew it. A response such as, "The CAO (or CFO) never advised us of this problem until it was too late to take any corrective action," has been found to be unacceptable to the courts. They view the governing body as having the mandate to be on top of such matters in order to protect their shareholders from negligence.

Thus, while increasing resources and attention have been applied to training and recruiting the finest administrations, it is only more recently that the need to focus some of those resources on the training of the governing bodies has become apparent and, indeed, pressing.

If the chosen model of governance is to stand the test of time, and the stresses of this rapidly changing world in which we live, the model must be based on certain key principles that are acceptable to corporate leaders.

What are the key principles of governance? While there may well be others, the following ten principles are essential to a sound governance system.

Principle #1: A Clear Mandate

Effective governance and administration requires the presence of a clearly established mandate set in legislation and local bylaws. Thus, the mandate of council to be responsible for the direction, actions and outcomes of the municipality's business must be clearly stated in legislation and well-understood.

As has been pointed out by many legal experts, there have been very real questions and concerns expressed about the lack of constitutional and legal authority for a municipality in Canada to do *anything* unless it has been granted that authority by its respective provincial government. The Constitution of Canada does not recognize local government as an order of government at all. Rather, municipalities are considered "creatures of the province" – if deemed desirable by the province. This has been both perplexing and frustrating to local governments across Canada, given that several existed before their provincial "masters," and given their significant responsibilities.

To some extent, that problem is now being addressed through new legislation that gives local governments *natural person powers*. The intent has been to increase the authority and powers of a municipality to the rights and powers of a real person, except where restricted by specific exemptions imposed by the province. While this has expanded municipal authority, it still leaves local governments struggling with their options and powers (including that of gaining access to additional sources of funding).

Council must understand not only what powers it possesses, but also what authority can be delegated to any operational or advisory boards and committees. Further, the powers of the head of council, and the mandate of that key position, must also be clear if that authority is to be exercised with real effectiveness. The head of council, as leader, needs to be provided with powers that facilitate leadership and the ability to focus the agenda of council.

This principle may also be applied to the management of the corporation. While our democratic base and history emphasize the leadership roles of the head and members of council, the supporting role of the administration must also be stated with clarity, and be based on principles that guard their professionalism and independence. In this instance, both provincial legislation and council's bylaws should send a clear message as to the responsibilities and accountability of the administration.

Principle #2: Clear Authority

In addition to understanding the legislated mandate of council and its members, associated committees, and the administration, the scope of authority of each of those roles must also be made clear. This authority may be conveyed by legislation, but will also likely need to be clarified by bylaws, policies and procedures.

Thus, the authority of council to set policy should be outlined. The role of council (and any standing committees) and the administration to advise (or decide) on those policies and to carry them out should also be conveyed clearly. Key areas requiring definition include:

➡ power to hire or release management employees;

➡ power to require work to be done and policies and resolutions to be carried out;

➡ power to delegate;

➡ power to approve expenditures and to what levels;

➡ power to over-ride a council-approved budget or reassign monies therein;

➡ power to appoint people to boards and committees; and

➡ power to change the reporting relationships of departments, etc.

Principle #3: Public Accountability and Responsiveness

An effective local government model (or decision-making system) must also reflect the basis of any democratic institution – a reliance upon the endorsement of the public. Council (and committee) decisions must be based on a clear sense of what is in the best interests of the public. As stewards of public trust, council and its institutions must be careful not to lose sight of the right of the public to be involved and to be fully informed.

In some respects, the governing body also has to be candid about what it can deliver and at what cost. Thus, council and its committees should be open to the public in terms of their decision-making processes to the extent practical, given the fact that certain issues may, for a time, be rightly judged as confidential.

At the very least, council's obligation of accountability to the public requires that it provide a regular means of advising the public as to its goals, objectives and strategies, and a subsequent report on how effectively those targets have been met. This can be accomplished through various means, including: a quarterly report; regular newspaper column; internal and external reviews of targets and progress; public access to the year-end results; open budget process; etc.

As well, council should advise the public as to how it can access council information, and provide input into the decision-making process. These mechanisms might include:

➡ public meetings of council;

➡ authority to appear as a delegation;

➡ "town hall" meetings held at various community locations;

➡ council documents made available at the local library or through the Internet;

➡ public hearings on matters impacting land use and major expenditures; and

➡ community roundtables on key issues (i.e. a shirtsleeves discussion).

Principle #4: Clear Sense of Purpose

Every organization requires a clear understanding of its purpose, as stated in its mandate, goals, objectives and strategies. This is essential if the organization is to maintain relevancy and focus, and be accountable for achieving its targets. In the municipal sector, such an understanding is often based on a step-by-step process – commonly referred to as corporate or strategic planning. This process must not only involve council and the administration, but also include input from the public. A broadly-based process of strategic planning involving the community can also be of value in ensuring that council recognizes the breadth of the issues.

Various mechanisms can be used by the corporation to ensure adequate public input, including:

➡ use of focus groups;

➡ public hearings;

➡ community forums;

➡ targeted representation from a cross-section of the municipality;

➡ council-boards-committees retreat; and

➡ surveys.

The key outcome should be a council-endorsed plan that reflects its commitment to certain short-term and long-range targets. These should be stated clearly, and include measurement criteria, where appropriate.

In order to be effective, such a plan must not only address the lofty aims of the municipality, but also specifically outline those objectives that are to be attained and when. Further, any plan that is intended to be more than rhetoric must point out specific responsibilities, so as to ensure appropriate action.

Principle #5: Full Disclosure

A basic principle of sound government is *access*. Council must have access to the necessary information it requires in order to make informed decisions. This is one of the components of a sound decision-making process, and is central to the level of confidence exhibited between council and its CAO.

Thus, council (and any standing committee) should be provided with:

➡ ongoing advice on the stated goals and targets of council;

➡ the best options available to resolve any business matter placed before council or one of its standing committees;

➡ updated reports on the handling of key issues;

➡ current advice on the fiscal health of the organization;

➡ status reports on any significant matter referred to the solicitors for action;

➡ a report on any significant matter in which the employment standards or security of the municipality have reportedly been breached; and

➡ reports that are comprehensive, yet succinct, and that are timely, so as to enable quality decision making.

It is essential that council receive the complete picture from the administration. Meeting this criteria ensures that no single, albeit organized, voice in the community is able to drive council's agenda.

Principle #6: Sense of Integration

Most municipalities are complex, multifaceted organizations that are involved with many issues and responsibilities. Given this breadth of scope, the municipality has the very real potential of reflecting confusion in purpose. It is important that the corporation, and its associated entities are all viewed as operating from the same page – that is, each must be clear as to accountability, reporting relationships, use of resources, achievement of results, etc. There must be a coherent sense of the whole organization, no matter what parts comprise the whole.

This implies that someone (generally the CAO) is responsible for setting the tone, and modelling a real sense of integration, such that groups, sections, divisions and departments are all on guard against duplication of resources and turf protectionism. Further, the CAO needs to encourage a high degree of sharing of information and resources, so as to avoid the misuse of resources in an environment focussed on results.

21

Principle #7: Sound Relationship Between Council and the CAO

The relationship of council and its standing committees (if any) to the CAO is critical to how well the system is run overall. This relationship must reflect:

➡ respect for the mandate and authority of each other;

➡ trust in commitments made;

➡ confidence in the word of each other, including the ability to handle confidential information appropriately;

➡ desire to help council achieve its mandate;

➡ willingness to implement decisions of council, even when those decisions do not reflect the advice of the administration;

➡ recognition by council of the professionalism of the administration, and its ability to get the job done;

➡ full disclosure of necessary information; and

➡ non-interference in allowing the CAO to get the job done.

Principle #8: Independence of Council

While council may receive input from a wide variety of sources (eg. committees, boards, external agencies, administration, public, developers, other businesspeople, external advisors, etc.), the act of governing is solely council's responsibility. And, while council may decide to delegate certain of its responsibilities to certain standing committees, the onus is still clearly on council to ensure that the organization is being governed appropriately. Thus, the policies, bylaws and resolutions of council are the mechanisms that must be used to bring about any action or course of direction. At the end of the day, the public holds council (including the head of council) accountable. This may result in a certain degree of frustration for council, in that it needs to have the authority to carry out its mandate in an atmosphere of public confidence.

There must be a certain independence being exercised by council. It must have the authority to seek alternate sources of input; to meet privately with independent advisors; to call in specialists from time to time to examine a certain matter; to be briefed by the auditor on the financial status of the corporation; etc. Council should exercise this independence within the boundaries established by legislation.

Principle #9: Orientation and Succession Planning

This principle reflects two related and necessary "bookends" of a sound governance-administrative system. At the outset of any council term, council members (including both returning and first-time elected officials) should receive a thorough briefing from the senior administration and any retained experts from outside the organization as to expected roles, relationships, powers, key issues, appointments, departmental overview, etc.

Similarly, council, as the governing body, should also be aware of its need for planned continuance. This requires council to develop a succession plan in the event of the departure of its CAO or other key personnel. Such a plan is not intended to designate someone to replace, on a permanent basis, the official who is leaving. Rather, the plan should identify the individuals who are to act on an interim basis, while a full scale search is launched.

Principle #10: Ongoing Performance Assessment

Any system or model of governance (and administration) must include a mechanism or process to ensure that it is performing as anticipated, and if not, that corrective steps are being taken. While it may be difficult for any governing body to conduct a self-assessment, it is not impossible, nor all that unusual. Council could – and should – use a written evaluative format at least once annually to serve as a "health check-up."

Such a process of self-assessment is often complemented by the annual report of the external auditor, who tends to focus on the fiscal policies, deliverables and public reporting and control processes.

The 10 Principles of Good Governance

Discussion Guide

1. *How do you see the role of governance as differing from the role of administration?*

2. *Where do you see areas of potential overlap?*

3. *How will you and your colleagues on council avoid interfering in administrative matters?*

4. *How important is a sound relationship with the CAO to you and your council? How will you go about establishing a solid relationship?*

Chapter 5

GOVERNANCE QUESTIONS

What kinds of questions do effective governing bodies ask? Obviously, the simple response is *policy questions*.

Policy questions strike at the heart of key governance issues, and refrain from delving into matters of day-to-day administration. They deliberately steer clear of involvement in the minutiae of administration (i.e. the "how does it happen" type of question).

The following is an overview of appropriate lines of questions, in various areas of governance.

Corporate Direction

1. Is the proposed course of action in line with council's approved corporate priorities?

2. How does this recommendation fit with previous decisions on this same topic?

3. When did we last communicate with the public regarding our priorities for this term/year? What was the response?

4. What does the most recent research tell us about the changing nature of our municipality?

Independent Advice

1. When do we review the appointment of our auditors? Our legal counsel?

2. What action can the CAO report with regard to follow-up on the auditor's management letter?

3. What date has been set for council to meet with the auditor?

4. What current information does legal counsel have with regard to any proposed legislative change?

Fiscal Issues

1. Do we, as a governing body, have a clear set of fiscal goals and priorities?

2. Does the present fiscal plan reflect our goals and priorities?

3. Do we have appropriate fiscal policies in place?

4. Do we have sufficient checks and balances in place to give us the necessary level of confidence?

5. What information do we have with regard to trends in terms of our fiscal position?

6. What might we learn from others in the municipal sector? What are we doing to ensure that we are on the leading edge of new developments?

Facility Management

1. What recent information do we have in terms of the condition of our municipal facilities?

2. Do we have a replacement plan and policy for each of our key facilities?

3. Has this information been built into our long-range budget planning?

4. What policy guidance have we provided to staff with regard to cost recovery?

5. Do we have an adequate monitoring system in place to ensure that any needy resident is taken into account?

6. Have we provided policy direction with regard to utilizing the private or not-for-profit sectors in the management or ownership of our facilities?

7. Are business and marketing plans needed, and if so, what is the process for developing such plans?

Government Relations

1. Do we have a clear indication of how our municipality is viewed by the provincial government, and how do we monitor that relationship?

2. What key issues do we need to gain provincial support for, and what do we envision as the major obstacles?

3.   What role does our head of council play in developing this relationship? How can the other members of council assist in this regard?

4.   What type of relations do we desire with our urban and rural neighbours? What areas of difficulty have we been experiencing in the recent past?

5.   Do we have a strategy to resolve any outstanding issues? Who is to take the lead on this dossier?

Program Development

1.   Have we reviewed our delivery of programs and services recently? What do those results tell us?

2.   Do we have a clear philosophy of our involvement in program delivery versus program facilitation?

3.   What significant changes have we made recently, and which changes do we presently forecast?

4.   When did we last survey the needs of our residents vis-à-vis programs? How do we factor in the changing demographics of our municipality?

Community Relations

1.   What mechanisms do we utilize to determine our rating with our ratepayers? Are they satisfied with our results and our behaviour?

2.   What mechanisms do we utilize to communicate with our residents? How do we know whether or not it is effective?

3.   Have we researched other kinds of community development techniques that have been used with any measure of success?

4.   Is there a communications plan to meet the organization's communication objectives?

New Initiatives

1.   How are we challenging ourselves as a council in terms of initiating new ideas for ensuring a constructive future for our residents?

2.   How do these initiatives fit into the strategic plan?

Risk Management

1.   What policies do we have in place to ensure that areas of potential risk are identified and properly addressed?

2. Have we developed a risk management plan to ensure that the administration takes the appropriate measures to reduce our risk potential?

3. Have we sought external expertise to ensure that our steps are appropriate?

Legislative Systems

1. Do our legislative systems reflect our preferred method of governance? Have we reviewed our systems recently?

2. What role do our advisory boards and committees play? What value do they add to the community?

3. How clear are our terms of reference for such boards and committees?

Transparency

1. What steps could we take to ensure that the decision-making process is publicly transparent?

2. Which decisions need to be discussed in closed meetings? Are we exceeding those limits?

3. What is the public perception of our openness to citizen input or criticism?

Professional Growth and Organizational Development

1. Do we provide adequate opportunities and support for the training of elected officials?

2. Do we aspire to be a learning organization? A smart organization? How are we doing that, and how do we assess our progress?

3. Has the CAO developed (or caused to be developed) a staff development plan that encompasses the full organization?

4. What is our policy regarding council attendance at conferences and seminars directly related to the business of the municipality? Are we able to determine which conferences and seminars are appropriate during the annual budget process?

5. Does our policy governing the issue of personal development for members of council and the administration ensure that we are adequately funding this important area?

Results

1.   Do we have a clear concept of what we expect as the results of our term of office?

2.   Did we establish our own objectives as a council at the outset of this term?

3.   How do we communicate our results to the public? How do we determine whether or not this is effective?

These questions speak to the role of council in being fully briefed on matters within the "position description" of a governing body. Thus, questions that seek to determine "how will you as administrators actually carry this out," tend to be excluded.

Further, it is recognized that most governing bodies stray into such areas from time to time. It should help the policing of such intrusions, however, if council is made aware of the differences between policy making and administration. Governing bodies must be encouraged to elevate their sights and focus on this critical aspect of governing. Without such a focus, there will be a tendency to take on the work of administration, thereby neglecting the important role of governing and leading.

Discussion Guide

1. *What features separate a governance question from an administrative question?*

2. *Why is it important to ask such questions during a council meeting?*

3. *What should you, as a council member, do if you are not satisfied with the response from the administration?*

4. *Discuss with those in your group some leading governance questions regarding:*

(a) budgets;

(b) business plans;

(c) community social needs;

(d) quality of infrastructure.

Chapter 6

UNDERSTANDING LEADERSHIP

The principal task of those governing organizations is to lead. This is often misunderstood and vastly under-rated. The key failure is the seeming inability of the "governors" to focus on the important challenges facing the municipality, and concurrently, to move away from the all too frequent fascination with administrative issues. What is not clear is whether or not the cause of this frustrating phenomena is the natural affinity of politicians to administrative matters, or the reluctance of administrators to release the governors to lead.

Leadership Components

Leadership requires the application of certain basic components, including the following:

Understanding the organization's reason for existence – While the answer might appear to be straightforward, councillors would do well to spend some of their initial energies developing a sound appreciation of the fundamental purposes of local government. What does the legislation of your province *require* a municipality to do, and what does it *allow*? How much of what the municipality is presently doing has simply grown with time, and what services are actually within the realm of existing legislation? These questions should be placed before the administration, along with the direction to provide a clear-cut, yet comprehensive response.

Focussing on targets – It should be clear that not all issues on the agenda are of equal importance. A council is asked to make decisions on both the mundane, as well as significant issues. The key questions for any council at the outset of its term of office are:

> What do you view as the major issues facing this community?

> What actions do you want the administration to address on a priority basis?

The answers to these two questions will help to determine the agenda of council for the first year, if not the entire term. While other issues will arise over the course of the first few months, and then throughout the term, a council would do well to remember the issues that were of concern to citizens at the outset. These will become matters on which the public will expect a report as to progress made.

Chapter 7 deals with how a council should tackle this important aspect of setting agreed upon priorities.

Shared commitment – A council is expected to lead with enthusiasm. It should be proud of the community and desirous of making it better. This can only occur when the full council agrees to the priorities, as noted above, and determines to apply the necessary resources of the community to have these issues resolved.

Part of being a leader in the context of local government requires an understanding of how to work together as both a council and administration to accomplish priority tasks on behalf of all residents. This necessitates a sound commitment between council and the administration to work together in a collegial fashion for the good of the community. There is little room left for egos and private agendas. Council and the administration must develop a common spirit of togetherness, while still respecting the very distinct roles played by each separate "arm" of government.

Accountability – Leadership is all about accountability. Unfortunately, there are many who enjoy the perks and prestige of leadership, but who shy away from accepting responsibility for decisions made and actions taken. Council should expect to be faced with some very difficult decisions during its term of office. These require decisions to be made. Not all of these decisions will be unanimous, and many may provoke considerable controversy.

While this may be so, residents presume they have elected a group of individuals who will have the capability to examine the issues, and make those choices that appear to be in the best interests of the majority of the residents of the community. Regardless of the resistance encountered, council members should still be capable of accepting the "heat" generated, and standing behind decisions they made with the available information. Council should re-visit a former decision (and possibly even reverse its stand) only when there is new information brought to the table.

Some issues are difficult. The resulting decision by council may seemingly divide the community. The fact that they are difficult should not inhibit a council from taking a stance on the issue. While referring it to the administration might be prudent if some information is lacking, continuing to refer it back for more and more information as a means of stalling the inevitable is not appropriate. The public understands that council will be faced with difficult choices from time to time. It also expects council to be capable of making a decision – even if some of the public believe it to be wrong or ill-advised.

When things do go wrong in the opinion of the community, council needs to have the fortitude to accept, both individually and collectively, responsibility for their actions. The best way to avoid having to admit to wrong decisions or inappropriate actions is to ensure that a step-by-step process of decision making has been followed.

Understanding the client – Defining who the client is for a municipal council would appear to be a fairly straightforward issue. Unfortunately, it is anything but a simple matter. The "client" may be the local businessperson, the senior citizen, the stay-at-home parent, the prospective businessperson, the land developer, and so on. Each may have a different agenda or set of expectations, which may be contrary to each other! The key question for council should be: "What is in the best interests of our community?" If this consideration is paramount in the minds of council members, then the resulting decision will be reflective of community interests.

Service delivery – Leaders occupy the positions they do because they are constantly looking for ways to improve upon the present situation. Most leaders are not *status quo* people. They want to move ahead of the crowd. Some leave public life when they sense that the challenge is no longer there, or that they are now more interested in defending what they did in the past. The former Premier of Alberta, the Honourable Peter Lougheed, was once quoted as saying, "The way I look at it is, some day I'll walk into my office and I won't be trying to change things. I'll find I'm trying to protect what I've done, and I know that's the day I'll start planning to leave."

Municipal leaders need to be constantly aware of how the present system and practices can be replaced by something better. In order to take real advantage of such opportunities, it is critical that both council and the CAO be onside and committed to the change process.

Delegation – One of the more significant changes in our society over the past 20 years has been the emergence of a "I'm not responsible" generation. For whatever reasons, we have created a generation with a sense of non-accountability. This has resulted in many people being unable to step up to the plate and accept either responsibility or authority. Part of the task of community leaders is to create a willingness and a recognition that real leadership is exercised by those who understand the principle of accountability. This necessitates the delegation of realistic levels of responsibility in municipal organizations, through bylaws, policies and job descriptions. Employees need to know the expectations of the organization in terms of work, results and timelines. It is inappropriate for either council or management to ease these responsibilities by interfering in the learning process. Such a process, albeit painful at times, is best experienced by the employee, rather than sheltered by the boss.

Acceptable behaviour – Given the attention accorded to the topic of mentoring over the past few years by both the secular and Christian media, most people are becoming more aware of the value of the organization's leaders establishing and personifying behaviour traits that are to be adopted by others in the organization. It has been my experience that values and ethics that are apparent throughout the organization are often a reflection of those exhibited by the leadership. Having recently worked with a municipality whose administrative leader was believed to have "fudged the books" relative to a minor matter, it was not surprising to find that several others in the organization were also carrying on very questionable practices (eg. misleading a member of council; engaging in intimate relationships with subordinate employees; opening private mail; misusing the municipal credit card). As some sage once remarked,"the fish begins to rot from the head."

Leadership Traits

While too much can be made of defining the traits that a leader must exhibit, there are definite leadership behaviours that enable elected leaders to be successful.

Among the most valued leadership character traits are:

➡ ability to communicate on a multi-level basis;

➡ adherence to the highest standard of integrity;

➡ willingness to hear the views of others, regardless of how divergent these are from the leader's own views;

➡ ability to search for and find areas of compromise;

➡ sense of what the community would see as important;

➡ willingness to stand alone in spite of the heat created by others;

➡ pragmatic approach to issues;

➡ understanding ear to those who others would set aside;

➡ vigorous defence of what is right;

➡ deference to others who are senior and more experienced in the matter, while being prepared to differ;

➡ compassion and willingness to forgive quickly and without reservation;

➡ persistence bordering on tenacity in pursuit of a course;

➡ ability to bring out the best in others;

➡ sufficient strength of character to accept blame for failures and to deflect the praise to others when success is evident; and

➡ confidence – an ability to communicate this to others as well.

Taking a Stand

Being a leader is all about being willing to take a stand for what you believe to be true. There are several keys, however, to ensuring that this is appropriate.

➡ Determine whether or not the issue is a "gamebreaker."

➡ Ensure that you have all of the relevant facts, so that your position cannot be seriously undermined and your credibility damaged.

➡ Examine the potential pitfalls in advance, and be prepared for these to occur.

37

➡   Enlist, if possible, the support of others.

➡   Attempt, if possible, to link the issue to other, perhaps more popular causes.

In order for a councillor to be successful, he or she must be capable of eliciting support from a majority of others around the council table. Otherwise, while it may be possible to embarrass the others, little concrete progress will be discernible. In fact, if the intent is simply to embarrass, then the prospect of future successes on other issues will be remote. Unfortunately, many councils have this kind of an individual on council – one whose only objective appears to be to gain notoriety as a disturber, and thus to be assured of re-election. This is based, perhaps, on the premise that the public believes every council needs someone on it whose main mandate in life is to torment others!

This is not to say that a councillor should refrain from taking a stand on unpopular issues. Indeed, if that is how the councillor feels or believes that others feel, then the stand should be vigorously defended. At the same time, however, the issue has the best hope for success if others on council see the proponent as someone who tends to make sense on most issues, and who seems to have a grasp on the will of the public.

Knowing When to Move On

When the issue has been put to a vote, however, and it fails to attract the necessary support, then it is time to move on to the next issue or cause. This recognizes, firstly, that in a democracy everyone is allowed to vote their own conscience. Secondly, it is recognized that a losing vote means the issue is defeated. And no, the others would not have voted with you if only they had more time or evidence; the result would have been the same. So, give it your best effort at the outset. Then, practice the adage, "When the horse is dead, dismount!"

Leadership Choices

Being placed in a position of leadership requires that appropriate choices be made, based on the values and principles of the individual. Such values and principles will often be challenged – and in ways that are often very difficult to predict or even to control. At the end of the day, what people expect of their elected officials is the ability to lead – to make wise choices that they believe are in concert with the will of the majority.

Most elected leaders are quite comfortable making choices in the following situations:

➡ where there is no real alternative (i.e. this is clearly the best choice, and it will be easily understood by the public);

➡ where the public is not present in council chambers to hear the arguments;

➡ on issues that are not in opposition to what personal friends would support;

➡ on decisions that can be used to gain the support of others on issues of greater importance to me; or

➡ where individual values are not at the centre of the argument (i.e. where the notion of what the individual really holds dear is not in question).

Quality leadership requires:

➡ ability to clearly discern issues and principles at stake;

➡ willingness to take a personal stand based on what is morally right;

➡ understanding of what would appear to constitute the public will;

➡ strength to resist the naysayers of the issue, based on a defensible position; and

➡ foresight to see the longer term impacts of the issue, and thus the willingness to stick with the decision in light of an alternative that would be immediately more acceptable, but an unwise choice in the future.

Discussion Guide

1. What do you feel are the key characteristics of a good municipal leader?

2. What qualities separate a leader from a manager? Can a CAO be both a leader and a manager? If yes, when might this occur?

3. How has your council tried to establish the principles of account-ability? Is it clear to you as to what the CAO is accountable for, and the accountability of the council? Are they both the same? Why or why not?

Chapter 7

ROLES OF ELECTED OFFICIAL
The Importance of Clarity

Municipal government is based on the principle of ensuring that residents have a voice in the affairs of their community that impact their well-being. This requires the election of people who are prepared to serve in leadership positions, and who are willing to exercise their best judgment on issues impacting the lives of others.

Remembering Our Roots

Who are elected officials? The day before the election, they were our neighbours and friends. They held work positions in various occupations, or were blessed with the ability to stay home with their families. Some have served in various avocations in the community such as the Lions Club, the Rotary, the recreation or library board, on a minor hockey staff, and so on. Others have spent their lives working in various business endeavours, and now find that they have time to make a time-intensive commitment to public life. Others have retired, and their spouses are finding their full-time presence at home more of a strain than a blessing. In the final analysis, elected officials are *us*!

The fact that we all come from such different backgrounds, results in each of us viewing this role quite differently. Some see the role of councillor as:

➡ an extension of their current job (or their boss's job);

➡ a variation of the Rotary Club or Legion;

➡ akin to the role of cabinet minister;

➡ the municipal ombudsman; or

➡ the judge!

All of the foregoing may be partially correct, but totally inappropriate if used as the model for this new role. That is to say, the role of council members involves an understanding of basic management principles; a desire to serve the community in a largely volunteer capacity; the need to make decisions similar to that of being a member of cabinet, and thus a team player in a caucus; a willingness to look into the issues that may affect only one or a few families, and seek some degree of resolution; and, finally, the readiness to render judgments without the wisdom of Solomon.

Why the Problem

The biggest issue confronting local government today is that of role clarity. The fact that this is so is likely due to a number of factors, including:

➡ unrealistic expectations of those being elected to public office;

➡ inadequate orientation of newly-elected officials;

➡ lack of understanding as to what governance is really all about;

➡ conflict between council and the CAO resulting in (or from) a lack of confidence in the ability of the latter to manage effectively; and

➡ overly aggressive and/or inquisitive members of council resulting in ongoing interference in the day-to-day management of the administration.

It is absolutely imperative that both council and the administration be aware of the roles that each is expected to play. Without such clarity, the roles are easily blurred, and serious problems result. As shown in the following diagram, the role of the elected official is complex and multifaceted.

While running the risk of over-simplifying this rather complex role, the following would seem to capture the key elements of those elected to govern our municipalities.

Leadership Role

Outline the future vision – While this role may seem self-evident, it is one that is frequently overlooked. Setting the vision does not mean simply endorsing the vision statement crafted by the previous council; nor does it mean accepting the glossy, professionally-crafted document presented to council by the CAO. If either of those steps were to be followed, it would provoke the question, So what difference did the election make? No, a new council (and *every* new term of office results in a new council) must set aside the time and engage in an appropriate exercise that enables council to discuss and debate "our" sense of what this community should be all about, and what priorities face the newly elected body for the coming term.

Set the priorities – One real danger facing each council is the sense that all issues are either equal or at least high on the list of priorities. This is clearly not the case. Regardless of how important someone makes the issue to be, it is up to council to determine the relative importance of the issues and their consideration. Given that council is the chosen voice of the electorate, it should be up to council to guide the setting of corporate and community priorities.

Uphold the laws governing the corporate and individual behaviour of council members – Unfortunately, each region of Canada has had its share of conflict of interest inquiries relative to members of council. Some are frivolous or minuscule, while others are substantive and troubling. The actual rules governing what constitutes conflict of interest are normally quite straightforward. Most municipalities generally offer access to the municipality's solicitor if an individual member of council is in doubt as to whether or not he or she should discuss or vote on a particular issue. A general rule of thumb goes something like this:

> If discussing the issue feels somehow wrong; if I feel that I may have an interest in this matter more so than the average citizen; and if voicing my views on this issue may cause others in the know to question my impartiality, I would not touch it with a ten-foot pole.

Councillors need to ensure that they not only act in the right interests and with the right motivations; they need to be *seen* to be acting ethically. For that reason, council should insist on a thorough briefing (preferably annually) as to their rights and privileges, as well as their personal and corporate constraints by experienced municipal counsel.

If a member of council has reason to believe that one of his or her colleagues may be in a conflict position, the moral thing to do would be to bring that to the individual's attention in advance of its consideration. If that would prove to be too difficult due to the current personal relationship or other factors, advise the head of council or the clerk. The most one can do, however, is *advise*.

Representational Role

Seek the input of the community on key issues – Ironically, some politicians believe that the public should only be consulted before the election – during the door knocking campaign – and then again prior to the next election. Eventually, such an attitude catches up with these politicians, who value public input only insofar as it gets them elected. It has been my experience that the public does not feel the need to become involved in all of the issues, but does appreciate the courtesy of being asked on those matters that are of key significance. An example of such matters might include: downtown redevelopment; amalgamation or annexation; building a new transportation corridor; allowing a hazardous waste complex in the city or on its borders; developing a new solid waste site; and so on. Such issues may only come up once or twice in the course of a term of office. Council needs to be aware of what the community would view as a "gamebreaker" and act accordingly.

Take issues forward on behalf of individual ratepayers – A further representational role played by members of council is that of acting as a conduit for citizens to have issues of importance to them considered by the appropriate body (i.e. council or the administration). Many people in the community will not fully grasp the niceties of protocol or accountability, and thus are inclined to contact "their" councillor directly regarding any issue that concerns them or their family or business. Whether the council member is the most suitable contact is not the issue. For the public, the council member is in a position of presumed authority, and thus better placed than they to access the right people to obtain a positive answer. Each council member should keep an ongoing list of such calls, so as to ensure that each has had a response from the appropriate source. The council member has the authority only to inquire as to the nature of the problem or question, and then commit to getting back to the individual. Any further commitment would likely be inappropriate or beyond the powers and authority of an individual member of council.

Conflict Resolution Role

Resolve differences on matters within the jurisdiction of the municipality – Generally, it does not take long for new members of council to realize that the bloom on the election night rose fades quickly. Quite frequently, council encounters a major and divisive issue very early into their term of office. Such an issue will either draw council together, or split them apart. Councillors will either gain an appreciation and respect for each other, or they will question the sincerity and authenticity of the remarks, questions and motivations of their colleagues.

In any event, resolving differences is the backbone of council's obligations. Council is expected to listen to all sides of the issue; seek administrative advice and research; review policy and budgetary consequences; ensure that a thorough process has been followed; and decide. The key is summed up in one word: *process*. If the appropriate process has been followed, then the decision rendered is far more likely to be acceptable to an impartial audience. Some councils still foolishly cling to the notion that they are expected to have all of the answers immediately upon hearing the issue. Thus, they attempt to respond to the request of a delegation on the night that they are first made aware of the issue. What nonsense! If they were asked to think through the following questions, their response might reflect a more sober assessment:

➡ Based on this presentation, what are our policy options?

➡ Do we have access to a considered opinion as to the flaws in this argument? Have we just heard one side of a story that has at least two, if not more, alternatives?

➡ If we say yes to this request, what precedent are we establishing for other similar requests?

➡ If we can make a decision on the spot, why do we employ senior staff, including a CAO, whose job it is to give us advice on all issues?

Policy Guidance Role

Establish the policies and bylaws necessary to put council decisions into action and to guide the activities and actions of staff – One of the principal tasks of an elected official is to initiate and/or approve policies that create the framework for administrative actions.

Ensure that present policies reflect current council's views – Every council inherits the policies of the previous councils. That one statement should cause all new councils to ask the administration for a complete review of current policies to see whether or not they are consistent with the thinking of the new council. It is incumbent on a new council to ensure that it has had the opportunity to assess all present policies that signal council's approval or endorsement of a certain stance, and then to take the steps necessary to amend those policies that are no longer consistent or applicable. This is not to suggest that the current policy bank will be found wanting. Rather, it strongly recommends that every new council needs to see what it has inherited in terms of policies, investments, structure, staffing and current practices.

Ensure that those issues delegated by law or policy to the CAO are, in fact, delegated – In some provinces, the relationship between council and the CAO is governed by law. That is, the CAO may have a legislated obligation to carry out the decisions of council, and to be the *only* employee of council ensuring that this is done. Thus, there is a requirement on council to delegate the administrative handling of issues to the CAO. The CAO, in turn, is accountable to council for ensuring that its policies are implemented and followed.

Role in Determining Service Delivery

Decide which services will be offered – Many members of council assume that services presently being offered are those that the legislation requires to be offered. This assumption should be verified. It may well be that a council is required to provide potable water, sewage disposal, road maintenance, solid waste disposal and so on. At the same time, the legislation across Canada is generally permissive in enabling councils to make choices about other services and programs that *their* citizens may want, but that another community may deem to be beyond their needs and expectations (eg. recreation programs and facilities, social services, airports, marinas, etc.). Each new council needs to determine what its citizens both want and need.

Determine the level of services – Council has a responsibility to establish the level of services that the community will provide. This is generally accomplished by council through the budget and by the administration through a thorough process of standards setting, program and resource evaluation, and business process engineering. The dollars allocated via the approved budget will reflect the level of service council feels is necessary and affordable.

Determine how these services will be delivered – It is up to council to determine the method of service delivery. That is, council may determine that the current method by which services are delivered is not satisfactory, and that alternative mechanisms should be considered. While council obviously has to be cognizant of the prevailing labour laws of the province, municipalities across Canada have found ways to enter into new delivery systems, involving the private sector, non-profit organizations, volunteers and partnerships (some with neighbouring municipalities).

Monitoring Results

Assess the annual results of the activities and projects undertaken by the municipality – There are two bookends to a council year. The first – which really should be concluded by early December of the previous year – is the establishment of the budget as part of a comprehensive business planning process. The business planning process should include the establishment of goals, objectives and priorities, which then leads logically to compiling and approving the budget. The matching bookend is the evaluation of results, which should occur at year-end or as close thereto as possible. If the objectives are outlined with clarity at the outset of the year and are described in sufficient detail, then the potential to measure with effectiveness will be enhanced. The actual assessment of projects and activities should be delegated to the CAO, who should be charged with developing a thorough process of evaluation. Council's role is to discuss and assess the CAO's evaluation, and determine what the resulting message is for the ensuing year.

Ensure that the decisions of council are properly discharged – One of the roles of council that is often overlooked is that of monitoring results. While councils make a multitude of decisions in a year, they seldom ask, "What was the outcome of our decision/action?" As a result, councillors are more likely to mutter that issues disappear in the black hole of administration, seldom to be seen or heard of again! The way to tackle this is to establish key targets and priorities at the outset of a given year, and then to put the onus on the CAO, perhaps through his or her performance review, to brief council on the results.

Fiduciary Leadership Role

Ensure that an appropriate and comprehensive budget process has been established – As outlined earlier, every council is expected to approve a budget on an annual basis. This instrument, together with a solid range of policies, gives council all the tools it needs to control the actions of the administration, and to direct the accomplishments that are expected by the community. In establishing the budget and subsequent mill rate, council signals what results are to be achieved, and the degree of tax subsidy by the residents/businesses of the community. To the extent practical, this should involve the community by providing open access to preliminary budget discussions.

Ensure that the external auditor has access to all necessary financial information, and monitor the administration's compliance with any recommendations – One of the mechanisms that council has at its disposal is the external auditor, who is charged with determining whether or not the organization operated within policies and budgets, and took steps necessary to minimize risks. While the value of the auditor is often overlooked, the auditor's intervention can be very beneficial. Council should insist on receiving a personal briefing by the external auditor as to the financial stability of the organization, together with a review of the internal controls, investment policies, variance reporting and financial management policies and practices. Council should then meet with the CAO to determine how and when council will be briefed by the CAO as to compliance with the approved recommendations of the auditor.

Roles of Elected Official

Leadership
- Vision
- Priorities
- Legislative

Conflict Resolution
- Resolve Differences
- Seek Alternatives
- Review Policy Options

Representational
- Community Input
- Community Advocate

Policy Guidance
- Review Policy Bank
- Ensure Currency of Present Policies

Establishing Service Delivery
- Determine Services
- Establish Level of Services
- Decide on Method of Delivery

Monitoring Results
- Set Targets
- Assess Annual Results
- Report Publicly

Fiduciary Leadership
- Budget Process
- Council Financial Policies
- External Audit
- Compliance

49

Discussion Guide

1.   *Please discuss the roles described in this Chapter. Are these the only key roles, or have you encountered others?*

2.   *Can an elected official make commitments to individual ratepayers? If so, what type of commitments can be made?*

3.   *Can you think of examples of services that could be discontinued? Any that could be initiated?*

4.   *Is it ever appropriate for an elected official to side with an element of the community that is clearly in the minority on a particular issue? How can an elected official really ascertain the will of the public on important issues?*

"Before we begin, let us take a moment to
reflect upon our hidden agenda."

Chapter 8

HEAD OF COUNCIL

The head of council, as chief elected officer of the corporation, can have a significant impact on how both council and management are perceived by the public. The head of council may variously be known as the mayor, chair, reeve, etc. For ease of reference (and without wanting to diminish other comparable position titles), the head of council will be referred to as the mayor in this Chapter.

The mayor has considerable power, albeit largely informal, and can exercise this influence over the conduct of the municipality's business. This does not ignore the fact that the mayor has only one vote on all matters and is, in many respects, co-equal with his or her colleagues on council. Rather, it reflects the fact that the public and media often tend to pay more attention to the mayor than to others on council. The mayor must therefore be very prudent in his or her use of this power, and should exercise it for the good of the community as a whole.

Need for Support from Council

The image of the mayor as an effective leader is highly dependent on the willingness of the rest of council to follow the lead of the mayor and to work together. This does not dispute the right of individual council members to have independent views on all topics. Rather, this observation reflects the need of council to receive leadership from the chair, and to respect the right of the mayor to provide such leadership to the fullest extent he or she is able to do so.

To be effective, the mayor will need to be able to solicit the agreement of his or her colleagues to work cooperatively on a commonly chosen gameplan. It is also expected that the mayor will encourage colleagues on council to view accepted policy from a "council as one unit" perspective, rather than individually.

There is considerable inherent value to the community in the role of the mayor – providing that this role is clearly understood, and providing that the incumbent has the presence (or force) to maximize this potential. Without behaving as someone with dictatorial powers, the mayor can establish a significant presence in the region and with the province by identifying and leading a change or reinvigoration process. The mayor must lead – and this requires a sense of personal vision for the future of the community.

Mayor as Political, Not Administrative Leader

In recognizing that the mayor is expected to be the political, not the administrative leader, much of the legislation across Canada requires council to delegate the day-to-day "administration" of the organization to the office of the CAO. This is based on two premises:

1.   The council is to hire a qualified administrator (CAO) who is capable of managing the corporation and community within council's guidelines and policies; and

2.   The mayor is elected as a political leader and as a representative of the people. He or she is not expected to have any training as a municipal administrator. On the other hand, the mayor needs to be able to understand community issues and concerns, and to be able to lead council toward a successful resolution of the key issues.

Principal Functions

The principal functions of the mayor can be categorized into the following four key groupings:

1.   Leadership Functions:

➡   chair of regular meetings of council;

➡   consensus-seeker on behalf of all members;

➡   key spokesperson to community and to municipal organizations;

➡   recommends the establishment of council committees and appoints members to both internal and external boards and committees; and

➡   makes recommendations re: peace, order, good government.

2.   Communication Functions:

➡   briefs council members on all meetings and correspondence;

➡   liaises with CAO;

➡ liaises with public;

➡ key linkage and spokesperson to other levels of government; and

➡ communicates decisions of council to outside world, expressing the will of council.

3.   Monitoring Functions:

➡ acts as council's eyes and ears in maintaining an overseeing role with regard to the conduct of municipal officers;

➡ recommends the suspension of a municipal officer or employee if necessary (note: this power is not held commonly across Canada); and

➡ ensures that the law is carried out (again, much of this is presumed to be delegated to the CAO).

4.   Representational Functions:

➡ acts in an *ex officio* capacity to boards and committees;

➡ performs a ceremonial role on special occasions; and

➡ main spokesperson to other levels of government.

Leadership Functions

This is perhaps the role most frequently seen by the public and by council alike. The mayor is expected to chair each meeting of council, and ensure that the business of council is handled expeditiously and effectively. This requires the mayor to be aware of meeting protocol, the concerns of his or her council members, the personalities of councillors, and the issues to be determined at that meeting. The mayor needs to be comfortable with power and with dispensing authority with clarity and equality.

He or she needs to be well-briefed by the CAO with regard to each and every agenda issue. The mayor should understand the basics of the issue; what is expected by the administration; the advantages of the proposed course of action; those who are most likely to be impacted; and what sort of public participation and/or reaction will be expected.

In most jurisdictions, it is not the mayor's responsibility to lead or guide the agenda process. While the mayor can request that certain items be placed on the agenda, as can the rest of council, the mayor, in most instances, is not expected to be in the position of screening agenda packages and determining what can or cannot appear before council at the subsequent meeting. This is normally the obligation of the CAO, whose job it is (by virtue of the *Municipal Act* and procedure bylaw) to ensure items requiring direction and resolution of council are placed before council in a comprehensive yet expedient fashion.

Appointments – With regard to the appointment of council members to boards and committees, it is normally deemed to be a prerogative of the mayor to recommend the appointment of council members on an annual basis. This prerogative needs to be limited by two caveats. First, the mayor should consult with all members of council prior to any recommended appointments being placed before the full council. Secondly, council as a whole should approve these appointments by a majority vote. Again, in some jurisdictions, this responsibility has been delegated to the mayor. Even so, it would be prudent of the mayor to have discussed this issue with his or her colleagues prior to making any final decisions.

This can be perceived as a fairly significant issue, and sometimes an emotionally charged issue given the desire by council members to serve on particular boards and organizations with which they have some personal degree of affinity. On the other hand, all members of council should be considered to be generalists on all issues, and thus should be eligible for appointment to all boards and committees. In this regard, it is wise for the mayor and councilors to reconsider this list of appointments each year, and ensure that some degree of rotation occurs during the course of a council term.

There is limited value in having the same councillors re-appointed to the same committees and boards year after year on the basis that having experience in those portfolios makes them somehow better councillors. Given that councils hire the expertise, is it necessary or even valuable to attempt to groom a councillor into a second expert? Councillors are expected to be the eyes and ears of the public – not an appendage of the administration.

Support for council's direction – As a leader, the mayor is expected to be capable of "rallying the troops" around a particular issue or course of direction. The direction, however, must be that established by the full council, rather than by the mayor individually. Thus, in some instances, the mayor may be obliged to pull the full council together towards a particular direction that the mayor may or may not have supported at the outset. This obviously requires someone with the ability to lead based on decisions established by consensus, rather someone who can only lead if the consensus reflects their own opinion. While this is a difficult matter, the mayor is nonetheless one individual who must be able to draw disparate views together and enable a consensus to be reached.

Likely one of the most difficult tasks of any mayor is the expectation that he or she will be able to find the common ground between councillors amidst the sea of diverse opinion. This task is daunting at times due to the disparate positions that may be vigorously held by other members of council. As the leader of council, the mayor is, however, expected to draw the views of colleagues together, and to point out a reasonable compromise if one exists. The mayor needs to remain impartial on the issue until it has been presented to council, and until it is appropriate for the mayor to voice his or her personal views on the issue. While the mayor is not expected to compromise his or her principles, most issues have within them the potential for agreement, provided that people are prepared to see each other's point of view. The difficulty, of course, is convincing everyone that some degree of compromise may be needed to reach a reasonable solution.

Perceived versus real power – The vast majority of the power of the mayor's office is more implied than it is stated. The office of the mayor carries with it considerable perceived clout in the community, given the status and respect most people accord to that office. While it may not have much additional formal power than that of any other member of council, the mayor is expected to be the leader of the community and to be capable of taking charge of the issues. The mayor also has an implied obligation to convey the will of council to the public, whether or not the mayor has actually supported the decision of council. The public needs to know what council has decided on a particular issue. This is a role the mayor is ideally suited to play.

Communication Functions

One of the keys to effective leadership as a mayor is the ability to ensure that council as a whole is well-briefed at all times with regard to the information that the mayor becomes party to as a result of his or her office. Council members generally understand that the mayor may become privy to information and/or concerns, given the mayor's leadership role in the community. While this affords the mayor with advance notice of such issues or even potential new projects, the mayor has an obligation to immediately inform council colleagues and the CAO as to the nature of such discussions. Indeed, it is preferable that the mayor strive to have either the CAO or the deputy mayor present in such discussions.

Prior briefing – Due to the prominence of the office, the mayor may often be briefed on issues prior to the rest of council. Such a briefing will generally come via the CAO and in some instances by virtue of the mayor's greater degree of access to other provincial officials and even the public. This additional access to information places the mayor under some obligation to ensure that the rest of council receives a full briefing of such issues, so that they are cognizant of all the relevant concerns and potential remedies. It is not wise for the mayor to ever withhold such information if council is expected to work together under his or her leadership. Thus, the mayor and the CAO will need to establish a mechanism that ensures all members of council are equally and concurrently advised of issues as they develop.

Spokesperson to administration – Due in part to his or her position as leader of council, and in part to the more frequent presence of the mayor in the office, the mayor is expected to be council's main spokesperson to the administration. This role is particularly important as a means of ensuring that the views of council as a whole are understood at the senior administrative levels. The mayor needs to be able to advise the CAO and senior staff as to council's anticipated view of a matter or to clarify a policy position or explain a particular grievance as expressed by council.

The mayor needs to be careful, however, that his or her actions do not lead the rest of the organization to conclude that the mayor is the administrator. The mayor, like all members of council, needs to defer to the CAO on staff issues, or run the risk of severely damaging and undermining that office. This is one of the reasons why the mayor needs to be careful in how accessible he or she is to members of staff other than the CAO, unless such meetings are held with the agreement of the CAO, or at least with his or her advance knowledge.

Monitoring Functions

The mayor has an implied obligation to monitor the delivery of local government services. This does not imply that any member of council, including the mayor, is to directly supervise the work of the administration. Rather, there is a responsibility to maintain an awareness of what services, programs and policies are being implemented, and to continually assess whether or not these are meeting community needs and standards. This can be achieved through simply being aware of what is going on in the community and bringing any issue that needs attention to the notice of the CAO. If the matter is within existing policy, the CAO will endeavour to act upon the mayor's suggestion, while if the matter is deemed by the CAO to be beyond present council policies, then he or she is required to bring such a matter back to the whole council at a duly called meeting for council's resolution.

Review of staff behaviour – In this process, it is possible that a member of council may believe that a member of staff has acted inappropriately. This should not result in the council member publicly criticizing the staff member. Rather, such a matter should be brought to the attention of the CAO to use his or her authority and act as deemed appropriate, given his or her assessment of the situation.

Regardless of the rationale for such criticism, there should never be any direct public criticism of the administration by any member of council. The mayor should immediately rule such comments out of order, and remind councillors of their commitment to this protocol. The appropriate place for negative comments vis-à-vis administrative performance, however, is in a closed meeting between council and the CAO.

Accessing advice – There also needs to be a clear understanding by all parties that the appropriate protocol for a member of council in accessing administrative advice (at a council meeting) requires referral of such enquiries to the CAO for his or her response. It should be up to the CAO to determine what response is appropriate, and whether or not he or she has sufficient information to answer the question, or whether the issue should be referred to another member of the administration. It may well be that the CAO recognizes that the issue is linked to several others that are under review, and thus the best response would be to defer any answer. Council should accord the CAO this courtesy.

Representational Functions

The mayor, by virtue of office, may be appointed to various boards and committees. These special purpose bodies (SPBs) may have been the creation of council and may consist, at least in part, of public citizens who are asked to advise the municipality on one or more key functions (eg. planning, recreation, tourism). The presence of the mayor is often sought when a group wants to:

➡ ensure ongoing support by council;

➡ increase the likelihood of council being informed as to the issues; and

➡ obtain some insight as to how council may react to a particular recommendation.

Need to reflect council's views – It needs to be made clear, however, that the mayor's role is to reflect the views of council (as they exist in terms of policy, resolutions, bylaws and informal debates/discussions) to the SPB. If the SPB presumes that it is hearing the word of council, only to find out that the mayor's opinion was very much a minority viewpoint, problems of credibility will result.

One note of caution must be underlined. The role of the mayor is to act as a liaison (similar to that of any member of council who serves on an SPB) or as a regular member. It needs to be emphasized that, unless the legislation provides otherwise, the role of the mayor or other member of council is not that of an advocate. The chair of the SPB should act as the advocate to council on any advice or recommendation provided by the SPB. Given that the mayor and/or other members of council will be considering the request in light of council policies and budget impacts, they must feel that their options have not been compromised. This would be the case if the mayor or councillor was expected by the SPB to be their advocate.

Ceremonial functions – Every mayor across Canada is expected, from time to time, to perform certain ceremonial duties. These can range from the annual parade to greeting the provincial premier on a speaking tour. Unless the mayor is otherwise committed, he or she is expected to be present and carry the civic colours. This tends to build a real sense of community pride and accomplishment. Thus, the importance of this role should not be diminished. While these events are important, not all need to be attended to by the mayor. Depending upon availability, size of the event and other demands of the mayor's office, the mayor may want to delegate such an appearance to another member of council. This delegation to individual councillors needs to be regularly rotated to avoid any appearance of favouritism.

As the official representative of the community, the mayor will frequently be the host for visiting groups and delegations. This will require the mayor to have some latitude, in that any expenses incurred by the mayor in hosting such organizations, delegations or individuals, should be legitimately picked up by the municipality. An appropriate record-keeping process, as recommended by the CAO upon the input of the external auditor, should be determined. A reasonable budget needs to be established for this purpose on an annual basis.

Representative to other leaders – The mayor is also expected to be the key representative of council in meetings with other municipalities (unless delegated to another member of council) and the provincial and federal governments. Any liaison on a political level should normally be conducted through the mayor's office. When another level of government is pondering new legislation or a new regional or local project, they expect to receive the opinion of council when dealing with the office of the mayor. While that role may be delegated on occasion to another member of council or a committee, it should, as a matter of protocol, be voiced and/or coordinated through the office of the mayor.

Need for Support

While the additional powers and prestige of the office of the mayor are recognized, these powers are only effective when supported by the rest of council. This serves as a useful check upon the authority of not only the mayor, but also council as a whole. There needs to be a genuine recognition of the value of working together and finding consensus on the issues. This will require respect for the right of each other to hold views that are at variance with others on council.

This respect should be conveyed not only at the council table, but publicly as well. That is, the public and staff of the municipality should not hear a councillor or the mayor publicly deride one of their colleagues, regardless of the circumstance. That would be unprofessional and not serve any constructive purpose.

Roles of the Head of Council

Leadership
- Chair of meetings
- Consensus-seeker
- Community spokesperson
- Speak to the issues
- Make recommendations
  - peace
  - order
  - good government

Communication
- Brief Council
- Liaison with CAO
- Liaison with public
- Key link and spokesperson to other levels of government
- Communicate "will of council" to public

Monitoring
- Guide/review conduct of CAO
- Recommend suspension of municipal officer if necessary
- Ensure that law carried out
- Review function of committees

Representational
- Act in an *ex officio* capacity to boards and committees
- Perform ceremonial role
- Main spokesperson to other levels of government
- Main spokesperson with media

Discussion Guide

1. *Please discuss the roles described in this Chapter. Are these the only key roles, or have you encountered others?*

2. *Can the mayor make commitments to individual ratepayers? If so, what type of commitments can be made?*

3. *How can the mayor lead without seeming to be dictatorial?*

4. *How often should the mayor meet informally with the rest of council to discuss their own problems regarding relationships, style of representation, attention to obligations, interference with the administration, etc.? Should this be done in a closed meeting?*

Chapter 9

COUNCIL LANDMINES

Many governing bodies are plagued by an inability to successfully tackle the problems that undermine their effectiveness. These problems or challenges are neither new nor unique to one council and not another. It is said that being forewarned, is being forearmed. Unfortunately, that popular adage does not always hold true.

What follows is a description of some of the more frequent or "popular" landmines that potentially await each council.

Becoming a Cohesive Force, Without Neutering Personal Agendas

Becoming a council team does not necessitate dropping all personal aspirations for this term of office. Rather, it implies being able to work together constructively and cooperatively in the pursuit of agreed-upon common objectives. Thus, if you feel you were elected on a "no tax increase" agenda, this should not stop you from being an engaged participant in any council discussions regarding other initiatives, or even new measures that may result in a tax increase. Your point may be that council needs to seek public approval in advance to any significant new initiatives that will have a potentially negative impact on the municipality's spending pattern or budget envelope.

No Real Sense of Vision

Without a road map, any destination will do. That pretty much sums up what council is facing if it has not articulated its priorities and objectives in advance of its actions. (I remember vividly the call from a municipality that wanted me to assist council in developing goals and objectives. I refused. There was about three months left in its term!)

It is somewhat unbelievable to realize that a council – supposedly made up of the community's leaders – has not taken the time to discuss what its members hope to achieve over the ensuing term of office. As a result, members are forced to re-read past minutes of council to determine whether they actually made any decisions that could be framed in language suggesting an overall pattern or framework.

Councils will always be confronted with a plethora of issues that they did not contemplate in advance of the term of office. This is the nature of local government. Unfortunately, if council allows that fact to scuttle any real sense of a vision and series of objectives, virtually any issue can be made to look important or at least urgent.

Mistaking Activity for Progress

While sitting in the foyer of the assistant deputy minister of municipal affairs, I picked up a municipal association journal from a neighbouring province and thumbed its pages. In the middle, I came across a rather impressive listing of all the meetings the board of that association had attended on behalf of its members over the past two months. It was a lengthy listing, covering two pages completely. The dates were all listed, as were the names of the board members attending, and the acronym for what they were attending. The only thing missing, as I contemplated these two pages, were the words *so what*? In other words, what difference did all this activity make? Councillors are often overheard telling others how busy they have been since becoming elected to council. While it may sound as though they are complaining, they are not. They are seeking comments such as, "My, I'm so fortunate to have a piece of your valuable time" or, "No wonder you were not able to return my phone call of last Wednesday." The appropriate question in response to such a comment should be, "So, what have you accomplished on our behalf thus far?"

Defining and Sticking to Roles

The lack of role clarity has confounded many organizations across Canada – and not just in the public sector. In the absence of quality training on governance and a thorough orientation, there is every likelihood that problems in maintaining some degree of role separation will continue. Agree, as a council, to become well-briefed as to the legal obligations of a council and its CAO, and agree to respect the turf of each party. Practise a "one employee" organization, and you will be well on the way to understanding this delicate balance.

Recognizing the Gap Between Resources and Public Expectations

The dilemma often facing members of council is balancing the demands of a public that expects council to hold the line on rising expenditures, and a public that demands that council do thus and so with regard to their favourite project or pet peeve. Being a member of council sometimes requires the response to be *no* or *not yet*. That may even be the case when indeed the member of council campaigned on that particular platform – only to find out that the budget choices mean postponing the desirables to deal with the essentials.

Public Criticism of the Bureaucracy

I hate to admit to this, but there are bullies on some councils. Their idea of sport is to fry a member of the administration by name in a public forum, realizing that there is little likelihood that such remarks will result in any lasting damage – to the member of council that is. The old "let's tie the can to the bureaucracy" theme may seem to win favour in some quarters, but it is short-lived at best. Many of the "thinking public" realize that staff are simply a reflection of their political bosses, and that any effective organization recognizes that it needs to work together to achieve desired results. Council relies on the goodwill and support of its administration to make progress. Demeaning staff efforts will not improve morale or efficiency and effectiveness. Most likely, the reaction will be less than enthusiastic support for councillors taking liberties with staff who are, by the nature of their employment, almost without avenues for rebuttal.

Balancing Public Demands with Personal Obligations and Needs

Former members of council should be called in to be a part of the orientation for newly elected members. They should be issued one challenge: speak to the problems of re-adjusting to *normal* civilian life. Better yet, consider inviting the *spouses* of those former council members! The general advice would be: do not neglect the truly important things in life in favour of those that play to your ego needs, but are of a short-lived duration.

There is a life after politics. It should be planned for and adjusted to over time, preferably not thrust upon you because you were defeated. The best plan is to achieve some degree of balance during your days as an elected person. Spend good time with your family – and avoid the trap of saying things like *quality time*, which is a euphemism for *a lack of time*. Do not miss annual holidays or special family events, such as birthdays, anniversaries, etc. Your life will (or should) go on after politics. Political roles do not.

Defining the Word "Public"

I recall a member of the council by whom I was employed referring to the *public* with whom she had spoken to about this or that issue. Other members of council would exchange knowing looks, being fully aware that this meant the lady who lived next door, who had become one of the few that the councillor could claim to represent. Her definition was a very narrow one. The challenge for council is to determine just who constitutes the "public." Walter Lippmann once wrote, "The public might be presumed to be that which [people] would choose if they saw clearly, thought rationally and acted benevolently." That is as good a definition as I have ever heard, and one that bears close reflection. It is not possible nor logical to expect to know the public will on every issue. What all citizens expect, however, is a council who attempts to reflect the will of the public as they understand it to be. Listening to local gossip and considering it as the "gospel" is a trap some council members fall into all too readily. Just because a staff member calls a councillor at home on the guise of sharing with the councillor "what's really going on" does not mean that the councillor is any better informed than before the telephone call. It may well be that you have just received an earful from a very disgruntled employee who has not been able to get his or her way with the department head or supervisor.

Further, the loud voices in council chambers do not constitute the public. They may be an aspect of it, or they may represent the mainstream opinion. It is council's job to make that assessment, and not those on the other side of the table.

Misusing the Position of Councillor or Mayor

Elected officials must constantly be aware of the extent and limits of their individual and collective powers. Without wishing to embark on a legal dissertation of such issues (for which I am not qualified), there are some "common sense" issues and comments that do pertain, as outlined in the following "Ten Commandments."

1. Thou shall not attempt to convey to others the impression that you have the power to decide issues that are not allocated to you by legislation or bylaw.

2. Thou shall not attempt to gain employment for a family member or for anyone else in the community. Let everyone follow the normal recruitment process and ensure everyone understands that such matters are the purview of the administration.

3. Thou shall not attempt to gain an advantage or favour for any company or organization in which you have any form of pecuniary interest, including a former role as an employee, shareholder or owner.

4.   Thou shall not attempt to coerce or convince the administration to undertake any action, program or initiative for which you do not have prior formal approval of council.

5.   Thou shall not commit the municipality to any course of action for which you do not have the formal prior approval of council.

6.   Thou shall not, in response to an inquiry from a member of the public, commit to any action other than "I will look into that and get back to you."

7.   Thou shall not leak information to friends, neighbours or the media if it has arisen in a closed meeting setting, wherein confidentiality of all such matters is required. Being privy to confidential information is an onerous responsibility. It is confidential for good reason. Having loose lips because of some desire to be seen to be either "in the know" or powerful, or because "the public has a right to know" is never appropriate.

8.   Thou shall not seek to undermine the authority of the CAO, nor do or say anything that would cause others to question the legitimate power and authority of the CAO.

9.   Thou shall not develop a close personal friendship with any member of the administration, so that you will always be in a solid position to evaluate their performance. Do not travel on holidays together; or take fishing trips together; or encourage your spouses to become best friends. When you have stepped down from public life, make your own choices in this regard.

10.   Thou shall not presume that the public "owes" you the next term because of your diligence and personal sacrifices this term. Each term requires that you seek the public's endorsement, not they yours.

As Charles Dudley Warner once commented, "Public opinion is stronger than the legislature, and nearly as strong is the Ten Commandments." (He was, of course, referring to *The* Ten Commandments. Still, the point is well taken here.)

Tolerating Incompetence

As stated earlier, council members should never publicly demean members of the administration. This does not mean that incompetence should be tolerated, however. This has been the death knell of some councils, and the plague of others. Councils across Canada must have a solid base of confidence and trust in those who serve them as their CAOs. This is essential to good government. Thus, while there must be sufficient time for CAOs to prove themselves to their new councils as worthy of support, there comes a time when a judgment must be rendered. This should be done with the use of a thorough evaluative process and, where necessary, with the assistance of experienced legal counsel. Take decisive action where it is warranted. Do not put it off. The situation will not improve.

Misunderstanding the Power/Roles of SPBs

Chapter 8 touched on the role and purpose of special purpose bodies (SPBs) and their impact on governance. Suffice it to say here that councillors should not misunderstand the legitimate authority of SPBs, nor ignore them, nor grant them the perception of power that rightly belongs only to council. Learn to listen intently and respectfully to their advice and, when appropriate, follow it. Ensure that the SPB's terms of reference are clear before establishing such a body, and ensure that mechanisms are in place in advance to change membership in such bodies on a regular basis.

Intolerance for Opposing Views and Absence of Personal Respect

Working in an adversarial environment is not pleasant for anyone. Meeting twice monthly (or perhaps more frequently due to a lack of concern for the time of others and their personal lives), is difficult enough without having the relationships so strained that the pervading sense of tension is evident before the meeting begins. Becoming a councillor does not necessarily mean the creation of a whole new set of friendships. On the other hand, it does mean the inheritance of a new set of colleagues. Given that you will be working together for the next 3 to 4 years (at a minimum), it would seem preferable to learn how to tolerate views that may be diametrically opposed to yours. It is possible to respect the right of others to differ while maintaining mature relationships.

Disregard for Protocol and Decorum

It would be nice to say that all those elected to public office were prepared to follow the rules of engagement – nice, just not true. The vast majority of those elected are able to function within the boundaries of the legislation, procedural bylaw, policies and commonly accepted decorum. As in most sectors of society or enterprise, however, it is not the vast majority who create the most problems. No, the high maintenance folks are those who:

➡ are convinced that the rules apply to the others;

➡ feel as though the world is out to get them (i.e. are looking to shift blame to others);

➡ have fractured or frail egos stemming from un-addressed hurts of their past, which are readily brought to the council table;

➡ were the grade school bullies who have simply taken their act to another playground; or

➡ never had such attention focussed on them, and believe in their right to be high maintenance.

It would be useful to report the great successes that various municipalities have had in coping with their problem children, but the literature is strangely silent in that regard. The mayor (unless he or she is the problem) can take the person aside and provide some timely counsel; recess the meeting if any obnoxious or undisciplined behaviour is exhibited; request a motion of censure by council; or ask to have the behaviour issue referred to legal counsel if that is warranted. It may not be wise, however, to expect a Saul-like transformation in the individual's performance. Unfortunately, the rest of council can become "tarred with the same brush" if other usually 'normal" members of council become inclined to engage in gutter warfare.

Losing Sight of the Client (Failure to Communicate)

The famous line in the movie "Cool Hand Luke" comes to mind. In that classic, the warden and his boys have caught up to Luke (Paul Newman) after one of his escapades – another escape attempt, as I recall. The warden is using his brutality against Luke as a show and tell and says, "What we have here is a failure to communicate." Unfortunately, one of the classic failures of governing bodies is simply that – a failure to communicate. One would think that politicians would be expert at knowing how to communicate with the public, and yet many fail miserably. Some rely on the media to do this for them, supposing that this is the media's responsibility. (Ask the media if you still are not sure of the answer to that statement.) Others hope that the interested public will attend council meetings. Some publish the annual financial statement, realizing that some people either:

➡ read everything; or

➡ find the examination thereof useful in combatting insomnia!

Communication should be viewed as one of the principal tasks of any public body. Some research into what others have done successfully should be the starting point.

Accountability and Responsibility

Finally, it is important for council to learn to make a decision and then stand by it. Do not be swayed by each gust of wind that blows contrary to the decision rendered. Be able to stand up and say, "We considered all of the relevant information that we were able to research on this topic, and we have made a decision." Seldom will someone point out the hidden topical information that you failed to consider. They may simply disagree – which is still permitted in a democracy. Share credit for the wins you and your council experience. Use the royal "we" when referring to such victories. Use the same terminology when stepping up to the plate for decisions that are criticized. Do not make reference to the staff report or the CEO's advice. Simply vow to keep improving and take the heat if necessary.

Council Landmines

➡ Mistaking collaboration for uniformity

➡ No real sense of vision

➡ Mistaking activity for progress

➡ Defining and sticking to roles

➡ Recognizing the gap between resources and public expectations

➡ Public criticism of the bureaucracy

➡ Balancing public demands with personal obligations and needs

➡ Defining the word "public"

➡ Misusing the position of councillor or mayor

➡ Tolerating incompetence

➡ Misunderstanding the power/roles of special purpose bodies

➡ Lack of tolerance for opposing views;

➡ Absence of personal respect

➡ Behaving without regard to protocol or decorum

➡ Losing sight of the client (failure to communicate)

➡ Being accountable

Discussion Guide

1.   *Please discuss the landmines described in this Chapter. Which of these have caused problems in your council?*

2.   *What steps are you taking to ensure that these are resolved?*

Chapter 10

COUNCIL-MANAGEMENT PROBLEMS

Clearly, there have been and will be problems between those governing municipalities and those charged with administration. Indeed, the single issue of role clarity has dominated all others as the greatest source of discontent between those elected to govern and those appointed to manage and/or deliver services.

Key Differences

The fact that there will be problems between councils and their senior administrations should really be anticipated. These two components of municipal leadership differ in many respects. For instance:

➡ council members are chosen from amongst the laypeople of the community, whereas administrators are hired based on their professional expertise;

➡ council members make decisions generally based on what they perceive as the wishes of the majority of citizens, whereas administrators make decisions and/or provide recommendations based on their academic training and/or experience as to what works best;

➡ councillors are elected for three-year terms (four years in Manitoba and Newfoundland), whereas administrators are generally appointed to positions that may span a full career;

➡ councillors are focussed on what they can achieve during the course of their term of office, whereas administrators may think in terms of the next 5 to 10 years; and

➡ input by the public to councillors often appears to reflect urgency, whereas the same input to the administration may be far less time-sensitive.

Style Differences

While it may seem relatively insignificant at first blush, the fact that council and the CAO have very different styles of operating, may lead to terminal problems in their relationship. Council members may have been elected on a platform of change in terms of how the municipality is to be governed and managed. The mood of the public, as expressed at the polls, may have been one of "it's time to aggressively pursue commercial development." The CAO, on the other hand, may be determined to stick with the policies of the past, which appeared to serve the municipality well, and which supported a "go slow" approach. The notion that this (or any) council is going to come in and expect rapid and 180 degree change is simply unacceptable. "Over time, council will see that I'm right."

Interference

While the principle of council being responsible for governing, and administration for managing, may be acceptable in some communities, it has not always "caught on" in others. Thus, some communities are still trying to find the appropriate balance between their council and administration. In certain instances, councillors may covertly be trying to direct staff without doing so through the CAO, while in others, the direction to staff may be far more direct and overt.

Abuse of Power

Unfortunately, no one sector of society has the exclusive hold on abusing their rights and privileges. Thus, the municipal field has had its share of those who have exercised raw power against people in vulnerable positions. Council members need to be reminded that their formal power must be exercised within the parameters of a council meeting. The fact that someone is elected immediately confers a sense of informal power – i.e. "I have access to power that you do not have, and I can get things done." While this may be true, it still requires convincing other members of council, so that a majority of council votes in favour of the proposition. Pretending to be powerful and in charge of the day-to-day affairs of the administration is both dangerous and corrupt. Such behaviour is the hallmark of the ethically-challenged and an omen of future problems.

Unwillingness to be Flexible

Political life is often a matter of compromise. Indeed, it has been defined as such. This requires an ability to be flexible on how issues are decided without giving up on personal ethics. Unfortunately, some people refuse to see the middle ground, and stand on theirs long after it has become apparent that the situation is untenable or unworkable. The sage politician makes a determined effort to see the arguments put forward by others in a reasonable light, and then determines whether or not the two positions are sufficiently close that some compromise may work.

Poor Communication

Like so many other aspects of corporate life, effective municipalities depend on open, transparent and comprehensive communication. This requires both council and senior management to commit to keeping each other regularly informed on all key issues. This works both ways. The CAO must see that it is his or her job to be completely forthright and open regarding when communicating key information and advice. Similarly, the CAO relies upon open communication with members of council, so that issues (whether of substance or not) can be dealt with quickly and in the proper context.

Lack of Confidentiality

A breach of confidentiality may or may not result in a significant loss of trust amongst members of council or between council and their administration. If the breach is accidental and singular, it is likely to be quickly forgotten, and hopefully forgiven. If the release of confidential information is intentional and/or repetitive, then there is a strong likelihood of long-lasting damage.

Confidential matters are reasonably limited and, in many municipalities, particularly smaller ones, not often on the agenda. The basis of local government is "public business being conducted publicly." Unfortunately, some members of council either practice that to a fault, or else believe all matters of any significance should be discussed privately with very little opportunity for public consumption. Neither stance is correct, nor lends itself to open and effective government.

Political Agenda of Administration

Where the administration becomes involved in political debate or political activity, the same type of problems arise as when councillors busy themselves in matters delegated to the administration by legislation, regulation or bylaw. That is, those people elected to office are offended by the behaviour of their staff, and respond – generally quickly and with actions that may spell the imminent end of an otherwise promising tenure in that community.

Disputes Before Assuming Office

Many of those who become involved in public life have had prior involvement with the municipality. They may have served on a local board or committee; become a member of a service or sports club; argued an assessment notice before the appeal board; represented a developer; or argued against a development. These experiences may have been very positive, and thus encouraged the individual to seek other ways of serving the community. Or, the encounters may have been quite negative, resulting in personal and perhaps public criticism being voiced.

In some instances, the citizen may have developed rather strong impressions of the staff he or she encountered, and then became the "boss" upon becoming elected. Unless the newly-elected official is able to separate the previous public contact from the new relationship upon which both have just embarked, tension between the two, particularly where there is reason for ongoing contact, may arise. In some instances, whether confessed or not (mostly not), the inability of one or another party to separate the two relationships has led to a career change.

Abuse of Trust and Other Unethical Behaviour

The ethics issue can cut both ways. That is, while abuse of public office is normally associated with elected officials, the fact of the matter suggests that administrators can also be guilty of misusing their powers and authorities. Such abuse can occur in various ways. For example:

➡ council might agree to keep a certain matter confidential, and then violate that commitment;

➡ a member of staff may misuse municipal power or spending authority, or may direct work to those with whom they are friends or close colleagues, or for whom such a favour may result in other favours being re-paid later;

➡ trips to out-of-town or out-of-province conventions can be used for personal business, or as a means of taking the family on vacation at the same time as attendance at the convention is expected;

➡ *per diems* can be charged, wherein no approval had been granted, or wherein the member did not attend the event or meeting except to register.

Role Confusion and/or Overlap

There are repeated examples throughout Canadian municipalities of politicians trying to act as managers, and managers assuming the rights granted to elected officials. This single issue has been the graveyard of many appointed officials. Typically, the source of the problem has much more to do with the presumption of those elected that they have been elected to manage. While this has its genesis in many factors, the degree of confusion at the end of the day can cause tremendous resentment and doubt relative to the motivation of both elected and appointed officials. Certain behaviour problems stand out:

➡ councillors (or the head of council) directing members of staff to do certain things;

➡ councillors (or the head of council) bypassing the office of the CAO and giving "guidance" to subordinate employees;

➡ councillors (or the head of council) committing to a member of the community that the municipality will take certain actions; and

➡ council members writing their own reports based on their attendance at external meetings, thus becoming employees or at least confusing the role to be played by the external agency (i.e. confusion about whether the member is an advocate, a member, an employee, the clerk, or a member of council who is to act as a liaison).

Lack of Clear Sense of Direction

In the absence of an agreed upon course of action, organizations simply drift. Decisions get made; work is conducted and fulfilled; staff are hired and replaced; meetings are held by the governing body; and the organization flounders. Someone has to establish the vision for the future and the priorities for the immediate present. This is generally presumed to be the role of council, although it is a role that needs to be shared with the administration if it is to be effective.

Each journey requires a destination. Each organization depends upon a sense of purpose. If council wants to ensure that the administration is serving its needs and working towards its goals, then time must be spent to ensure that these needs and goals are articulated. Councils cannot presume that the administration can ascertain its collective will if this has never been articulated. Without any discussion and direction for change, the administration has no other alternative but to follow the policies and bylaws as established by prior councils. How ironic when you consider that many councils are elected on a platform of change. It is the responsibility of the elected council to determine the corporate gameplan. While the administration should be involved in a supportive role, the key lies in the degree of council ownership of the ideas.

Misunderstanding of Powers and Authority

Legislation, regulations, bylaws, policies and contracts establish who has the authority to do what. These statements need to be carefully reviewed so as to ensure that all parties are clear about role distinctions and prerogatives. Thus, there needs to be clarity relative to the power to:

➡ hire and fire;

➡ spend money or authorize its expenditure;

➡ engage contractors and consultants, and to authorize their terms of reference;

➡ establish boards and committees;

➡ speak to the media, and to authorize the release of information;

➡ set levels of compensation;

➡ approve promotions;

➡ waive fees/charges; and

➡ contact the government, and at what levels.

Lack of Accountability

One of the key elements in any effective organization is a clear sense of who is accountable and for what. Unfortunately, municipalities often allow or encourage a sense of shared accountability, to the extent that real accountability is never fully established. Thus, we see instances of councils or individual councillors becoming involved in the hiring of staff, both at the senior and junior levels. I recall the example of a council whose policy required members of council to be involved in all hiring of supervisory and management staff, as well as to be informed as to the names of those applying for lesser positions. In fact, the CAO was requested to send out a list and description of all applicants for a department head position, so that the councillors could rate each one (with no written criteria), and thus determine the short list! What ultimately happened, of course, was the CAO became almost incidental to the hiring process, and therefore neither responsible nor accountable for those hired.

Lack of Feedback Processes

It is essential that both administrators and councillors have some form of feedback mechanism, so as to relay a performance assessment. Without a formalized system of performance assessment, there is a strong likelihood of poor performance carrying on unchecked and/or solid performance lacking positive feedback. Indeed, employees often complain that they desire, but seldom receive, feedback as to their performance on the job.

While a part of this issue lies in managers lacking the discipline and understanding necessary to provide feedback, another key aspect of this lies in the totally misleading forms used by managers and councils alike to conduct appraisals. All too frequently, these are borrowed from other organizations and lack any semblance of relevance to the municipality in question. As a result, many supervisors still rate their employees according to some weak format that requires the appraiser to fill in the appropriate blank squares (often 1-5 or poor through excellent), without any substantiating comment or rationale. The answer for supervisors, of course, is to choose the rating in the middle, so as to avoid having to either fire the poor performer or reward the good employee.

Lack of Policy Direction

The lack of a "policy mindset" by a council and/or its administration produces many results, including:

➡ treating each issue, regardless of how common, as *new* or a *one off*;

➡ referring everything of any consequence up to council for their consideration;

➡ slowing the decision-making process to a snail's pace; and

➡ ensuring that decisions made are often inconsistent with those made on the same or similar issues recently.

Policies are as essential to an effective organization as blood is to the human organism. They provide the life and drive of the system, and enable those administering the organization to respond quickly, confidently and intelligently to the demands of the public. In lieu of any changes by council to the current policies, the administration should act as though all policies not rescinded are still in effect. (That statement alone should encourage a new council to get off its duff and review the current policy bank pronto!)

Discipline Lacking

When well-known personnel problems are left unattended and unresolved, it becomes apparent that the CAO is not fully in charge of the administrative organization. While these issues may be difficult to address, they do not fade away from inattention. What does happen, in many instances, is a growing awareness of the CAO's lack of ability to make tough decisions, even when staff are aware that these issues are begging to be re-solved. This lack of decisiveness by a CAO will also inevitably impact the assessment by council as to his or her performance.

No Sense of Integration or Coordination

Municipalities generally function with a minimal degree of administra-tion. As a result, they can ill afford duplication or overlap in order to pre-serve someone's perception of what they need to feel important or special. Thus, departments with a singular mandate are quickly being replaced with multi-functional departments.

As well, councils are beginning to examine the use of single purpose com-mittees, recognizing that they contribute to a misuse of staff resources and the splintering of council's focus.

Lack of Management Skills

It is unfortunate but true that some municipalities still suffer under the ad-ministrative guidance of those who reflect the "Peter Principle" (i.e. they have risen at least one rank above their level of competence). This failure will have a direct negative impact upon the municipality's ability to meet the expectations of either council or the public, or both. All too often, un-fortunately, it is left to fester amidst the fond hope that the individual in question will seek opportunities elsewhere (although such a hope is sel-dom realized). The lack of such skills shows up in many ways, but often in light of a poorly-handled major issue, or a staff revolt, or ongoing depar-tures of the quality and portable staff. At times, the situation has to become almost desperate before council is sufficiently convinced that they have run out of options.

Unfortunately, the municipal field has not sought ways of actively devel-oping quality managers and supervisors; thus, there is a diminishing bank of first-rate CAOs and senior staff available for some very attractive posi-tions. Contributing to this issue is the fact that many municipalities insist on paying paltry salaries to qualified candidates, preferring to find the least expensive – and, consequently, the least qualified, or least likely to make a difference.

Instant Expert Syndrome

One of the easiest and most common traps of an elected official is presum-ing that the process of becoming elected also conveyed, through some im-mediate process of osmosis, an ability to understand all issues and be con-versant with all of their nuances. This, of course, also conveys the impression of immaturity and a decided lack of understanding as to role expectations. Unfortunately, this syndrome is frequently aided and abetted by staff who fear their new masters, and are concerned that any briefing, regardless of how straightforward or how in-depth, will be greeted with sarcasm and the impression of "we already knew all of that." Even when that is so, particularly for returning members, it is wise to expect and seek the administrative briefing. To repeat: **Council members are not expected to be the expert. That is what they hire.**

Discussion Guide

1. *The potential exists for problems between council and management of every municipality. Have any of the problems described in this Chapter affected yours? If so, how?*

2. *How do you attempt to avoid these kinds of problems?*

3. *Who is responsible for ensuring that discipline problems experienced by the administration are being properly addressed?*

4. *If a member of the public calls a councillor demanding an explanation as to an existing policy, what stance do you adopt – that of an advocate; a defender of the status quo; a conduit to council?*

"Please note that the views in this report do not reflect that of management, and may affect the sensitivities of some members of the listening audience."

Chapter 11

GOVERNANCE "BEST PRACTICES"

While the term "best practices" has been overplayed recently, there is value in attempting to describe practices that signify and describe local governments that truly understand their roles and responsibilities, and that are trying to govern as effectively as possible. While these are similar to the "Hallmarks of an Effective Councillor" outlined in Chapter 12, they are written in a broader fashion, given that these apply more generically to council as a whole.

Building Blocks of "Best Practice"

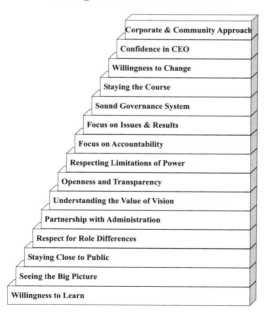

Corporate & Community Approach

Confidence in CEO

Willingness to Change

Staying the Course

Sound Governance System

Focus on Issues & Results

Focus on Accountability

Respecting Limitations of Power

Openness and Transparency

Understanding the Value of Vision

Partnership with Administration

Respect for Role Differences

Staying Close to Public

Seeing the Big Picture

Willingness to Learn

Willingness to Learn

Elected officials need to adopt a continuous learning mindset. This is a new role and one that is continually changing. Council members should be open to a process of ongoing training and development that focuses largely on their role as governors of the system. Such a mindset and commitment bodes well in terms of building a council that recognizes the enormity of the task at hand, and the importance of continuous learning.

Seeing the Big Picture

In order to truly add value to the future of the community, council members need to have the ability to see down the road. What impact will this decision have on future choices? If we do this, what policy consequences might we envision? How does this decision fit with our approved business plan? An effective council will attempt to put a whole picture together that addresses its vision, values, goals, objectives and issues. Regardless of the approach used by council, the key lies in the results being fully owned and endorsed by council, and not simply the baptism of a nice, glossy document carefully constructed by the administration, or worse yet, by an external consultant. "The Corporate Gameplan" should reflect council's view of the big picture.

The Corporate Gameplan

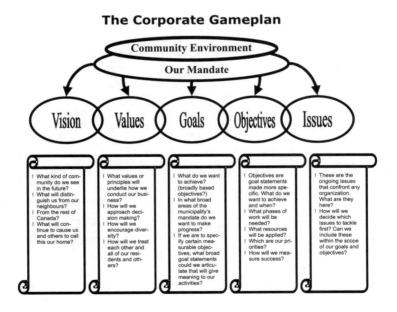

82

Staying Close to the People

Political leaders stay current to the extent that they are able to reflect the will of the public. This requires an ongoing presence with the public, and a willingness to hear decisions challenged, as well as applauded. An open and responsive council is not achieved by a council that meets by itself so frequently that it hears only its own voices and opinions (and that of its staff), and not necessarily what the public wants. New and creative ways must be found to ensure that decisions are grounded in public opinion, and not personal preferences.

Respect Role Differences

Quality people who are elected or appointed to office soon realize the reality of role distinctions, and the value of such differences. As a result, they work hard at their own roles and respect the responsibilities and accomplishments of their counterparts. Regardless of the inclination to "help out" with the functions of the administration, councillors are wise to focus on their own responsibilities. Public accountability is only served when the distinction between key roles is enhanced, and not blurred.

A Partnership with the Administration

In addition to the foregoing, a best practice in governance is the presence of a partnership between council and its administration. Such a partnership must be developed on a daily basis. In order for council to be effective in connecting with its public and fulfilling its campaign obligations, it must ensure that a close linkage has been carefully and respectfully developed with the administration. While individual council members can be effective from time to time on a specific issue, their "success" is generally short-lived without a concurrent connection with the administrative leadership.

Effective councils recognize the absolute requirement to value the role played by the administration, and to take those steps necessary to build a strong and lasting bridge. While respecting role differences, strong governing bodies work diligently at building linkages of mutual respect with their senior administrations. In each instance, this requires an acknowledgement of the need to channel all requests through the CAO. Such a partnership also builds on the knowledge that the administration is comprised of people who are very gifted in areas that are essential to the effective running of the municipality.

Vision and Priorities

Effective councils have articulated a vision of the preferred future of the municipality. More appropriately stated, they have found a mechanism to ensure that the public has worked with council and the administration in identifying goals and preferred objectives and strategies that, taken together, will assist in achieving the kind of community desired.

In moving towards that vision, it is worthwhile to note that not all issues are of equal importance. While that may seem apparent, it does seem to take some time for the message to sink in. Council will be faced with a plethora of issues in the course of its term. The key is to develop a corporately-endorsed mechanism for sorting out the important from the urgent, and the "game-breakers" from the mundane.

Openness and Transparency (Respect for Democracy)

It is fairly easy to argue that local government is the best form of government because it is most transparent to the people. It is quite another matter to ensure that all citizens have a reasonable degree of access to their elected leaders. One of the keys to building confidence in council is an expressed willingness, followed by ongoing practices that support open government. Council needs to be extremely reluctant in moving issues to a closed meeting. Public business needs to be done publicly.

Respecting the Limitations of Power

Becoming an elected official can be a very exhilarating experience. In many instances, the elected official realizes that this is the peak of his or her influence and status in the community, and a much more prestigious role than any other previously held. Unfortunately, not everyone is as interested in hearing the extent of their new power, and certainly not the fact that they hold little added personal authority (in the formal sense), but considerably more as a member of a collective body. And yet, even the collective body of council has many restraints and constraints on its authority, guided largely by the legislation applicable in each province. An effective councillor takes the time to understand those limitations, so that no abuse will be permitted or willingly incurred.

Accountability and Integrity

One of the surest ways of causing long-lasting damage to the ability of the municipality to function effectively, is to negate the need for clear accountability. If the CAO is responsible for the recruitment, development and supervision of the administration, then involving council in choosing who the next head of that important department is to be will blur the responsibility and accountability of both the CAO and department head. Thus, when problems arise, and they inevitably will, holding someone to account will be a fruitless exercise. Accountability requires a clear definition of responsibilities, and this is one hallmark of a "best practice" municipality.

Issues and Results

Councils tend to fail miserably when they lose sight of their mandate at the outset. Council members are elected due in large measure to their ability to articulate a message that the community "buys into." In some cases, it may be "a community open to business." In other locations, the campaign message might be "preserving our natural environment." Whatever the key message, a wise council will ensure the new focus is placed squarely on the issue, with the expectation that results will be delivered over a reasonable time frame. Thus, not only is the focus on key issues important; development, and then measurement, of the results are also essential. What do we expect to achieve? Over what time frame? What difference will this make?

The loss of focus by council, while mystifying perhaps, is usually quite simple to explain. Some council members believe the reason they were elected was, well, so that they could be elected. That is, "I've arrived." Unfortunately, the desire for change may be arrested at that point. Thus, the remainder of the term is spent supporting and justifying all administrative decisions, past and current. As a result, the real council agenda may never be articulated. Council members need to remember that they were elected to do something – not simply to perpetuate the *status quo*.

Sound Governance System

Decisions are made as a result of a process (and, sometimes, in spite of the process or lack thereof). The range of processes that a council might undertake in making decisions are numerous. Again, councils inherit a governance model. That is, a range of standing committees (or a committee of the whole) and special purpose bodies in place when the new council takes over. Unless the new council decides for whatever reason that the current structure and decision-making process does not fit its style, it is likely that the system that served the past council will continue.

Any change to council's decision-making system will only evolve from council itself. The question to ask is this: Does the present way by which decisions get made serve the needs of this council or not? Does the current system enable good decision making or frustrate it? After a brief period in office, each and every council should be asked that question by its head of council.

Stay the Course (Leadership on Tough Issues)

Council is often faced with a tough issue within its first 3 to 6 months. The peace that reigned to that point amongst council may be threatened. Sides may quickly be drawn. Emotions may be expressed. Personalities, rather than issues, may come to the fore. If council does not have a carefully considered process of decision making in hand, the lack of same will become readily and often painfully evident. A council that has ensured the process has been comprehensive, and the relevant issues properly aired, will usually make the "right" choices. Inevitably, these will be challenged. The successful council will not over-react to external pressures, particularly not where a thorough process has preceded the decision. The fact that councillors receive negative feedback at home or on the street, or by the media, does not mean the original decision was wrong.

Willingness to Change

Leadership embraces and embodies change. Best practice recognizes that we live in a rapidly changing world requiring our civic institutions also to change in order to keep pace.

I recall a conversation with a new councillor who had left a political career in local government 25 years earlier. As we walked through the municipal office on our way to the appointed room for our interview, he turned to me and said, "Do you know how this place has changed over the past 25 years?" I replied that I didn't. He responded, "The furniture is 25 years older!" In other words, nothing else of any substance had changed. Those in leadership positions had decided that their mandate was to simply maintain the previous course, in spite of many indications that change was in order.

Whenever considering a new way of doing business, the first question often asked is, "Who else does it this way?" The best advice is: If it is not illegal, and you have said you want to be a leader, why not make the change? You cannot lead by following someone else.

Confidence in Head of Council

Even amongst a group of leaders like those elected to council, someone must lead. In the case of a council, that leadership is expected to emanate from the office of the head of council. Unless the head of council is acting as king and grand potentate, successful councils should expect sound leadership to be exercised by this individual. This may be done quite vocally or quietly, at council meetings or in discussions with individual councillors and the CAO. The way by which the head of council provides leadership will be dependent upon the personal style of the incumbent. It must be done in terms of offering ideas and suggestions, because the head of council does not have unbridled power. This position is one of influence. How that is played out will determine how successful the head of council will be.

Unfortunately, in some communities, council is not even sworn into office before some member of council decides that the public has made a mistake, and that it is up to that councillor to make that evident by undermining or ridiculing the head of council for the next three years. This is both unprofessional and immature. It is also demeaning to the public, who have spoken through the ballot box.

Corporate and Community Approach to Issues

Effective organizations recognize and respect the fact that issues exist in a multi-functional and often interdependent context. Quite often, issues that might have appeared as "stand alone" at the outset, turn out to have significant interconnections to other functions within the organization, and perhaps even to other external organizations as well. For that reason, it behooves elected leaders to guard against any decision-making structure that would place an over-reliance on a strictly "departmental" approach.

As well, any involvement by an external body should be based on a multi-disciplinary approach, rather than narrowly defined special purpose bodies, whose focus is far too specific. Similarly, all issues presented to council should be preceded by an interdepartmental review coordinated by the CAO. Such a review is vital in ensuring that the views of all senior staff are reflected in council (or committee) matters prior to any discussion by elected officials.

Sadly, some municipalities provide for department head meetings the day after council meetings, rather than a week before. Such an approach results in a careful, though largely useless, review of what happened at the council meeting.

Discussion Guide

1. What mechanisms has your council employed to ensure that it is in a continual learning mode?

2. What mechanisms does your council use in ensuring that both council and the public feel connected? What can be done voluntarily by council in terms of encouraging public involvement in the business of the municipality?

3. What mechanisms does your council use in ensuring a healthy team approach with your administration?

Chapter 12

THE 12 HALLMARKS
OF A SUCCESSFUL ELECTED OFFICIAL

Not everyone elected to public office at any level of government succeeds. Many quickly become frustrated and are happy to leave after one term; others toil on in obscurity, either failing to ever have "their" agenda successfully addressed, or constantly heading the list of "best whines." Some are absolutely shocked by how little personal power they wield, while others are dismayed by how much time it takes to change policies or legislation.

Fortunately, many are highly effective and successful, adding greatly to the community's progress and improvement in the style of living. They work well with others and are pleased to see their community take even small steps of progress. What distinguishes those who are effective from those who are not? Without wishing to appear overly simplistic, it appears that there are 12 seminal characteristics of *effective* local elected leaders.

1. Prepared to Learn

Those rare individuals who are naturally brilliant do not always make successful or fulfilled elected leaders. Part of the reason lies in their inability to understand that this is a very distinct role from that found elsewhere in society. Preparedness and openness to learn that role is essential to success.

2. Servant of the Community

People who put their names forward for elected office are, generally speaking, doing so out of a love for their community and a willingness to serve. Often, they come out of a service background, having spent time and energy in volunteering for this or that community agency or club. They may have coached a minor hockey team; or served on the executive of their church; or taught dance classes; or laboured with the chamber of commerce.

3. Respectful of Others

Effective council members understand the need to listen respectfully to the ideas of others. While not necessarily quiet by nature, they are mature and courteous, recognizing that their colleagues have an equal right to state their views, regardless of how wrong or poorly articulated their views are! Such members of council become more effective by listening to how the positions of others are articulated, to see if there is any room in their views for compromise. While they do not necessarily endorse the views of others, they listen politely. This is a somewhat rare commodity, as most people are quickly formulating their own responses and trying to "one-up" the previous speaker. While this may appear as a "win" in the eyes of the speaker, it is short-lived and not designed to win supporters for the long haul.

4. Well-prepared

One of the first impressions that impacts a new councillor is the sheer volume of reading that is expected. While some of this may be unnecessary and designed to befuddle rather than illuminate, the requirement to do a lot of reading, in addition to other aspects of preparation, is evident. In some instances, it may require a drive past a certain intersection or work-site. In other instances, a visit to a particular neighbourhood or attendance at an "extra" meeting may be of value. All of these elements are aspects of preparation for council meetings. The lack of same becomes very evident to both staff and council and, at times, to the attending public. Asking questions at a council meeting does not always suffice, particularly when the answer to the question appears on the next page of the briefing materials that are thus far unread and untouched.

5. Understands and Accepts Democracy

It is a funny thing about democracy – most people are in full agreement with it until others disagree with their perspective. That is, while most people readily accept the premise that four beats three, being one of the three brings that premise into question. "How could they not see this simple issue my way?" cries out one of the dissenting voters at a council meeting. Not content to understand *no, they did not see it your way*, the proponent of the idea tries various other approaches, including bringing the topic back to council for its re-consideration. If that fails, browbeating the opposition or ridiculing their thinking is unsuccessfully attempted. Some have even either quit council or become antagonistic to the other non-believers. A child with marbles, walking home, is the picture that comes to mind.

6. Prepared to Ask "Dumb" Questions

I believe it was the great management thinker Peter Drucker who once explained that the role of board members was to ask dumb questions. Further, he explained that there was no such thing, because every question by a member of a governing body was probably on the minds of other members who were too timid to ask. Secondly, through asking questions, governing bodies make better decisions, because managers and advisors become more experienced and prepared to give more comprehensive advice.

7. Understands Teamwork; Resists Groupthink

Because councils are comprised of such different people, they often struggle with the notion of teamwork. Some dismiss the effort because of the obvious differences between the members, which may become apparent even before election results are known. Others determine that they are naturally aligned with what appears to be a winning coalition; thus, the need to seek the cooperation of others seems less urgent. Over the course of a term, however, councils change and individual councillors find that their position has moved much closer to those who originally appeared to be in another league. As Charles Dudley Warner remarked in 1870, "Politics makes strange bedfellows!"

Teamwork is important if a council is determined to make continuous progress. It requires the willingness to compromise on ideas, without the betrayal of principles. Teamwork necessitates a willingness to share the credit for good ideas, and an ability to show how the success for one can also be experienced by others. It needs to be differentiated from "groupthink," which is a term used to describe the pressure felt to agree, even when other views are strongly held. That is, an individual councillor may feel so much peer pressure to come alongside fellow councillors that he or she succumbs to their persuasion to do so. This is dangerous, and does not serve the interests of the public. The public understands that the election of a group of 5 to 15 councillors (depending upon jurisdiction and size of community) does not imply solidarity of thought. Indeed, many expect the sparks to fly on particularly ideological issues, and so they should. The key is the ability of individual councillors and the head of council as chair, to keep the disagreements to the issues at hand, and not focussed (as they too often are) on the personalities.

8. Prepared to Work

The challenge of becoming elected, quickly shifts in focus the day after the election. It is then that the workload that accompanies the role becomes more apparent, sometimes to the amazement of the new councillor. In many communities, the responsibilities and time commitment of a councillor are far more onerous than that portrayed prior to the election in the briefing materials made available to all candidates.

Effective members of council accept the obligations that elected office imposes, and quickly take on the expected requirements of background reading and meeting attendance. As well, new council members should ask questions relative to what elements of being on council are really essential, and those that are simply historic (i.e. appointments to boards and committees that are not useful or central to the municipality's core businesses). It is somewhat ironic that these appointments occur so soon after an election, when new members are ill-prepared to question their value or necessity.

9. Ability to Stay the Course and Sound Enthusiastic

Every so often, I am questioned as to whether or not there should be fixed term limits on how long any council member can *or should* serve. While I would generally argue that 2 to 3 terms of office should allow most people to make a contribution to their community and still be open to new ideas, there are some people who are able to stay effective and open-minded for a longer period of time. Thus, it would be to the community's disadvantage to have such an individual disqualified from continuing to render service. While this may never change, I would, on balance, argue in favour of allowing two four-year consecutive terms prior to requiring a one-term hiatus from the same office before re-offering.

It should be noted here that only a couple of provinces have seen the light and moved to four-year terms – and secondly, that the author served for four three-year terms before recognizing the value in giving the public a break from his performance!

10. Accountable

Effective council members understand the principle of accountability. They accept not only the accolades, but also the responsibility for tough and perhaps unpopular stances and decisions. I recall a former mayor of a neighbouring community publicly placing the blame for the community's precarious financial condition and foolish investment decisions on the CAO. That, in my view, was both immature and unfair, given that it was council who made the decision to buy up various parcels of land and initiate a whole new economic corridor. Regardless of where council gets advice and information from, it is *council* that is ultimately accountable for policy decisions.

11. Multi-Dimensional

Effective members of council are not "one trick ponies." That is, they recognize their need to expand their knowledge base into new dimensions and areas of community involvement. For a number of reasons, a new member of council should be discouraged from serving in areas close to their former profession or avocation, and placed into roles on boards and committees or task forces that require a completely different skill set or base of knowledge. This philosophy, which will likely meet considerable opposition, is based on the belief that a councillor is elected as a generalist, and should be so at the end of his or her term as well. Council members should develop an expertise in leadership and governing – not in public works or finance.

12. Personal Integrity

Without integrity, there is no value or substance. The true value of an elected official can be answered by one simple question: Is this a person who keeps his or her word? Do not make commitments that you later find convenient to break. Do not say that you will not be seeking more of an honorarium for your public service, and then join a chorus that claims the workload is beyond that imagined, and thus an increase is long overdue. You might come to that realization during a term of office. If so, and you have already claimed that the honorarium paid to the last council was sufficient, simply recommend a reconsideration and review by your council towards the end of its term, with any recommendations to be implemented on the first day of the new term. Further, if you make a commitment to another councillor to support an item, or the administration to support their proposal, and you learn of new information between that commitment and the decision date, call those to whom your commitment was made and advise of your change in plans. (A much better process of course, is to always refrain from such commitments in advance of hearing the debate around the council table and any additional input that might be brought forward by the administration or by the public.)

Begin and end your career as a person of integrity. At the end of the day, little else will matter.

93

Hallmark of a Successful Elected Official

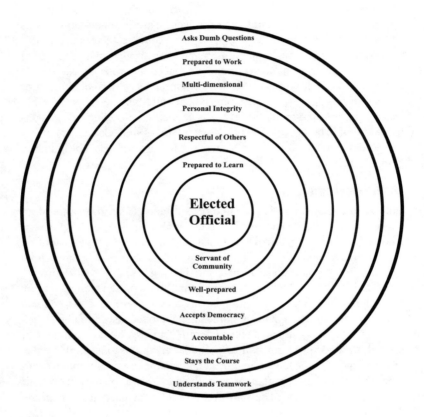

Discussion Guide

1. *What factors (both personal and situational) lead some members of council to presume that they are expected to be instantly familiar with all of the issues?*

2. *In your opinion, is there ever a situation that justifies abridging or violating the commitments of a council member to council as a whole?*

3. *What if you do not agree with keeping a certain matter confidential? Is that an area where you would feel a council member could violate a trust?*

4. *Do you take exception to the notion that council members should not become specialists in any subject matter of the council's mandate? What if a career or professional background prior to election to council parallels that of a department or function of the municipality?*

5. *How can council deal with councillors who are not keeping up their commitments, such as attending meetings of designated special purpose bodies?*

Epilogue

This has not been written as an all-inclusive or authoritative text on local government. Rather, it is intended to provide a compilation of thoughts around what works and what does not, as viewed by someone who has worked for, served as an elected official in, and acted as a consultant to various municipalities over some 30 years. Some of these thoughts have obviously been formulated while reviewing or being a part of what appears to be successful and, equally, seeing or participating in examples of significant failure.

As anyone who has written a text such as this will understand, my mind is racing ahead to a next volume wherein I hope to share some additional thoughts on what changes can and *should* be made.

I have a love for this calling at the community level where decisions directly impact lives, and a respect for all those who serve there with a sincere desire to make a difference.